Protect Your
Achilles Heel

🔲🔲🔲🔲🔲🔲🔲🔲🔲🔲

Also by Wess Roberts

Leadership Secrets of Attila the Hun

Straight A's Never Made Anybody Rich

Victory Secrets of Attila the Hun

Make It So (with Bill Ross)

Protect Your Achilles Heel

CRAFTING ARMOR FOR THE NEW AGE AT WORK

Wess Roberts, Ph.D.

ANDREWS AND McMEEL
A Universal Press Syndicate Company
Kansas City

Protect Your Achilles Heel: Crafting Armor for the New Age at Work copyright © 1997 by Wess Roberts, Ph.D. All rights reserved. Printed in the United States of America. No part of this book may be used or reproduced in any manner whatsoever without written permission except in the case of reprints in the context of reviews. For information, write Andrews and McMeel, a Universal Press Syndicate Company, 4520 Main Street, Kansas City, Missouri 64111.

Library of Congress Cataloging-in-Publication Data

Roberts, Wess.
Protect Your Achilles Heel : crafting armor for the new age at work / Wess Roberts.
p.   cm.
ISBN: 0-8362-2176-1 (hc)
1. Leadership. 2. Industrial sociology.
3. Psychology, Industrial. I. Title.
HD57.7.R6324 1997
650.1—dc21   96-48267
CIP

For Justin,
Jaime, Jeremy,
and Cheryl,
all of whom are
good forces in my life

CONTENTS

Contents

ACKNOWLEDGMENTS

IF I LISTENED to the urgings of pride's inner voice, I would attempt to take credit for this book in its entirety. But as that would be foolish, dishonest, and unappreciative, I will confess to a tremendous amount of encouragement and assistance in writing it.

First, I want to thank my agent and friend, Artie Pine, for suggesting the idea for a book on Achilles and for believing I could relate the truths of ancient Greek mythology as lessons for managing in the twenty-first century. Thanks to my other agent and friend, Richard Pine, for placing this book with Andrews and McMeel, a company he rightly described as making some serious innovations in the publishing world. I am also grateful to my comrade and confidant, Lori Andiman, for placing this book with publishers in other countries around the globe and for handling its audio and other subsidiary rights. Thanks, too, to Sarah Piel for her cheerful and competent administrative assistance from start to finish.

I am particularly grateful and privileged to have had Christine Schillig as my editor. She saw what this book could be long before I did and helped nurture it until I finally understood. I appreciate her patience, guidance, and enthusiastic support.

Ellen Roddick's line editing made a substantial improvement to my first draft. And then, just when I was feeling pretty proud of the manuscript, along came Catherine Whitney with a lesson in humility. Indeed, Catherine, with the help of her editing partner, Paul Krafin, found more flaws in my thinking and provided more remedies than I care to admit. Thanks, Catherine.

As I am no longer an executive with lots of coworkers on whom to impose my ideas, I now rely on executives, entrepreneurs, and professionals who live near me as my sounding board. Many thanks to Doug Hansen, Randy Staples, Chett Paulsen, Kevin Rose, Marcel Chappuis, and Michael Sullivan for their encouragement, criticisms, and suggestions.

Much appreciation goes to my family for their encouragement and assistance. Cheryl has never failed in her unique ability to keep me focused on the task at hand nor been anything but unselfish when I am writing. Jeremy was my principal technical adviser on Achilles and Greek mythology, having read the *Iliad*. (My prior knowledge of Achilles came from a quick scan of *Cliffs Notes* while driving to high school the morning I took a test on the Trojan War.) Justin was in Italy when I first began this project. On his return, he helped clarify many of the principles contained in it. And then there is my only daughter, Jaime: She provided me the motivation to work through every challenge that presented itself.

Last, but certainly not least, my thanks to all of you who buy this book. You make it possible for me to do something I enjoy, and I hope the lessons found here may help you in some small way to achieve a destiny that far exceeds the limits of your fate.

Attila's Camp
Sandy, Utah
October 1996

AUTHOR'S NOTE

THE STORY of Achilles has been
retold many times since Homer
wrote the *Iliad*. The myth, as
related here, is true to the
common interpretations
of the story. Any
modifications are in
the interests of drama,
and to place a greater
spotlight on Achilles.

CAST OF CHARACTERS

THE EPIC TALE OF THE TROJAN WAR involves a wide cast of characters. The following list includes those you will meet in this story.

❂ ACHILLES: The central character in the drama. Achilles is the son of the goddess Thetis and the human Peleus and has succeeded his father as king of the Myrmidons. Unequaled as a warrior and a great hero among the Greeks, Achilles suffers from a fatal mortal flaw.

❂ AGAMEMNON: King of Mycenae and supreme commander of the Greek forces during the Trojan War. Agamemnon is Achilles' superior.

❂ AJAX: A battlefield commander for the Greeks during the Trojan War. He is second only to Achilles as a hero and warrior.

❂ APOLLO: One of the twelve Olympian gods, the son of Zeus and Leto. Apollo is the god of light, reason, inspiration, the arts, prophecy and oracles, and healing. He takes the side of the Trojans during the war, and it is he whose arrow fatally pierces Achilles' heel.

❧ ATHENA: The Olympian goddess of wisdom. She stays Achilles' hand when he is enraged by his leader, Agamemnon.

❧ BRISEIS: The beautiful young maiden awarded to Achilles as a prize of war. The pivotal point in Achilles' story occurs when Briseis is taken from him by Agamemnon.

❧ CHIRON: The wisest and most famous centaur. Chiron was charged with raising the young Achilles and tutoring him in the arts of life, strength, and skill in war.

❧ CHRYSEIS: The daughter of Chryses, a priest of Apollo. She is taken captive by the Greeks and awarded to the supreme commander, Agamemnon, as a prize of war. When Apollo sends a deadly plague to decimate Agamemnon's army, Agamemnon is forced to return Chryseis to her father but takes Achilles' prize, Briseis, in her stead.

❧ HECTOR: Elder son of Priam and Hecuba, King and Queen of Troy. Hector is the mightiest Trojan hero and the supreme commander of the Trojan army until he is slain by Achilles in an act of revenge.

❧ HELEN: The daughter of Zeus and the mortal Leda, the most beautiful woman in the world. While married to Menelaus, King of Sparta, she is seduced and willingly abducted by Paris, who takes her to Troy, an act that starts the Trojan War.

❀ MEMNON: King of Ethiopia. Memnon and his army come to his uncle Priam's aid in the final days of the war, and Memnon is slain by Achilles.

❀ MENELAUS: King of Sparta and husband of Helen. After Helen is abducted, he declares war on Troy and appoints his brother, Agamemnon, as supreme commander of the Greek armies.

❀ NESTOR: An aging Greek hero, known for his wisdom and truthfulness. It is Nestor who tries to mend the rift of alienation between Agamemnon and Achilles.

❀ PARIS: Younger son of King Priam and Queen Hecuba. He is the abductor of Helen.

❀ PATROCLUS: Achilles' dearest and most devoted lifelong friend. He dies fighting in Achilles' place.

❀ PHOENIX: Friend and adviser to Peleus, Achilles' father, he helped Chiron tutor the young Achilles and became a Greek hero during the Trojan War.

❀ PRIAM: King of Troy.

❀ THETIS: A goddess of the sea and mother of Achilles. Thetis devotes her life to protecting her son from harm.

❀ ULYSSES (known as Odysseus in the Greek): The King of Ithaca, known as a man of great cunning. It is

Ulysses who masterminds the building of the wooden horse that brings the Trojan War to a close.

❦ ZEUS: Supreme deity and most powerful of the Olympian gods. Zeus is god of the sky, storm, lightning, and thunder. He is responsible for the fulfillment of fate's will.

	The Nine Flaws of Achilles	The Nine Shields of Immortality
Disloyalty	Commitment
Greed	Selflessness
Hostility	Cooperation
Betrayal	Integrity
Withdrawal	Rigor
Inflexibility	Flexibility
Deceit	Honesty
Vengeance	Respect
Arrogance	Humility

Protect Your Achilles Heel

🔲🔲🔲🔲🔲🔲🔲🔲🔲

INTRODUCTION

Achilles: A Modern Metaphor

ACHILLES MAY seem like a strange choice as a model for today's business leaders. Back in 1985, when I used Attila the Hun as a metaphor for leadership (*Leadership Secrets of Attila the Hun*), many people had the same reaction: What could a ruthless barbarian teach us about leadership?

Attila was a good teacher because the secret to his power was in his intuitive intellect, not in his savage intent. The lesson in leadership was Attila's ability to mold the uncivilized hordes of Huns from fractious clans into a nation capable of defeating the most disciplined and sophisticated armies of the civilized world. Attila was determined, tough, and dogged—an intriguing leader. He dared to stand and take command, even in the face of seemingly insurmountable odds. I recognized in Attila many of the qualities that are essential for leadership.

Times have changed since then. The messages of strength, daring, and beating the odds have taken solid root in our business culture; these values are still encouraged today. But attitudes and behaviors are not static. As the environment in which we do business changes rapidly, new dangers present themselves. We are living in a period of phenomenal growth and opportunity, but its blinding light can dazzle and mislead us. We risk forgetting the fundamental principles on which to build a solid foundation for lofty ventures.

Powerful metaphors for our current dilemmas burn vividly in Homer's epic tale *Iliad* and in other stories from cultures and civilizations long vanished. The eternal verities remain to light the way for us, to reveal our possible futures as they were so clearly written in the past. There is a simple reason why stories such as the epic tale of the Trojan War have remained prominent in our literature and language. They provide clear messages about the ongoing human quest for ethical, moral, and social guidelines in a world no less confusing than it was millenia ago.

The mythic Achilles, greater than mortal man but not quite god, is a fascinating example of how great promise can fall victim to moral failings. Achilles' heel has endured for centuries as the metaphor for bearing a fatal flaw—the chink in the armor that permits the tip of an arrow to penetrate and kill. If the vulnerable heel were the demigod's only flaw, perhaps we would be moved less deeply by his ultimate fate. But Achilles failed to appreciate his other very real vulnerability—his humanity—and in the process he fell victim to the dark side of that humanity. The Trojan War seemed almost to have been created as a showcase for a warrior of Achilles' skill and power. Yet he refused to join with his allies in battle against the enemy, brooding over personal insults. By sulking, Achilles wasted his considerable powers. His withdrawal from the field of action threatened more than his name. Angry and rancorous, he was chiefly concerned with his bruised feelings. Unable to master himself, he failed to use his great skills and lost his ability to protect himself.

We are left to wonder: Had Achilles adhered to the Olympian truths, had he shielded his mortal weakness, had he been as focused and as pure in life as he was on the battlefield, would he have succumbed to the same dark fate? Perhaps the god Apollo's arrow might not then have found its infinitesimal target, the little patch high at the narrow of the heel, that brought the demigod down.

As you will discover, Achilles is an ideal metaphor for the current crisis that faces our corporate world, in big companies and small. Achilles' promise is *our* promise. His flaws are *our* flaws. Are we to be numbly led on, ruled by fate's ruthless destiny? Or can we recognize familiar patterns and rise above the dark side of our own brooding mortality?

Is it possible to learn from the flaws and failings of Achilles and craft ways both to survive and to thrive in the new age at work? We shall see. But first, the story.

The Tale of Achilles

The sea nymph Thetis was one of the most desirable of the Olympian goddesses, and Zeus coveted her. But when an oracle warned Zeus that Thetis would give birth to a son who would exceed his father in power, Zeus spurned her. Neither his son nor any other would surpass the great Zeus! To guarantee that the oracle's prophecy would not threaten the Olympians, Zeus decreed that Thetis marry a mortal. She was wed to Peleus, king of the Myrmidons, and bore his son, Achilles. Achilles was destined for greatness, but not as a god.

Thetis was bitter about the blow to her child's destiny, and she plotted ways to endow him with the godly powers she believed were his birthright. Hoping to make her child invulnerable even though he was part mortal, she took the infant to the river Styx and plunged him into its magical waters.

But in her fervor to keep the child from being swept away, Thetis neglected to let the waters lap over Achilles' tiny heel, which remained untouched by the river. This fateful error left Achilles open to his ultimate mortality. His destiny was not to be an invulnerable god, as his mother dreamed, but a demigod, part mortal offspring of King Peleus of Myrmidon, and part god, son of the sea nymph Thetis: beloved of Zeus, but not of his world.

Soon after taking her child to the river Styx, the marriage of Thetis and Peleus collapsed. Leaving her son's tutoring to the wise Phoenix and the noble centaur Chiron, she devoted herself to protecting Achilles from harm, masking her son's mortality.

As he grew to young manhood, Achilles was fed the entrails of lions and wild boars for strength and bear marrow for courage. He learned the ways of nature and the seasons. He was tutored in music and singing, art and poetry. He was schooled in the art of healing and given the wisdom of the ages. Achilles also excelled in the many arts of combat, as well as in sports and horsemanship. A strong, sensitive, well-rounded, and balanced youth should emerge from such a rich education.

But Achilles was not just a noble youth, a royal prince. As Chiron and Phoenix constantly reminded him, he was not a mere mortal. He was also a demigod, favored of Zeus. Achilles swelled with pride at the notion, but the delicate balance between mortality and immortality was hard to maintain. The scales of his ego seesawed and then tipped toward godhood until he found it hard to believe he was of human blood. The arrogance of the demigod grew in him. He walked the earth, but he knew he was not entirely of the earth. He was able to create an aura of both superiority and invulnerability. The resulting gravitas made him the center of any group. But his naturally assumed arrogance was actually Achilles' base flaw—a core hubris from which all other flaws sprang. Achilles was never able to accept his humanity. Ironically, that denial of his mortality only made him weaker. Had he been able fully to accept his human half, perhaps the anxiety he felt at almost but not quite being a god would have been greatly reduced, and he could more readily have accepted the acts of men as being unmitigated by godlike prescience or command. Achilles, able to converse with the gods and have them intercede directly on his behalf, saw his life as lived on a higher plane. He radiated a different life force—stronger than any man, lesser than any god, but powerful—crackling with intelligence and energy. He was known and admired among all the Greeks. At every festival, at every funeral competition, at every game, at every battle, Achilles proved himself the greatest of warriors. Agamemnon, Menelaus, Ulysses*, the giant Ajax, Diomedes—all tested their skills against Achilles in friendly competitions and sport, and no one could surpass him.

When Helen, the beautiful queen of Sparta, was abducted by the Trojan prince Paris, Helen's enraged husband, King Menelaus, appealed to the Greeks to join him in a war against the Trojans to recover her. Menelaus appointed his brother, Agamemnon, to be the supreme commander of the Greek armies. Knowing of Achilles' unsurpassed skill in the arts of combat, Agamemnon implored him to join the war against Troy, and Achilles agreed. It is at this point that we first begin to detect flaws in Achilles' character.

Barely had he vowed loyalty to Agamemnon than his mother, Thetis, persuaded him to break his promise and flee his commitment. When he was discovered in hiding

*Also known in Greek as Odysseus.

6

and pressured to return to fight he did so, but still without any strong feeling of commitment to the goals of the Greeks. From the outset, Achilles was faithless to both the leader and the mission. Having easily broken his word once, he did so again. Stung by what he perceived to be an unfair decision and a grave insult from the leader to whom he had never been faithful, he reached to the gods for retribution, indifferent to the suffering he might cause his friends and allies. Wrapped in a cocoon of self-pity, Achilles set aside his weapons and sulked in his tent, even as a bonfire of combat blazed all around him. When finally his dearest friend, Patroclus, implored him to rescue his dying colleagues, he stubbornly refused; when finally forced by Patroclus to act, he did not himself rejoin the battle but allowed Patroclus, the friend he loved, to dress in his armor and fight in his place. When Achilles learned that Patroclus had been brutally slain, he was enveloped in wrath, mad with grief, rage, and anger. Only then did he finally emerge to do battle. But he was not inspired by any loyalty other than the loyalty to blood vengeance. Achilles had long ago forgotten the mission. His only desire was to kill the man who killed his friend. He wanted revenge; he was no longer concerned with victory over Troy.

The story of Achilles' role in the Trojan War, culminating in the fate that awaited him at the gates of Troy, is the keynote of an epic tale. In the end, the god Apollo, favoring Troy, let fly a poisoned arrow at Achilles' vulnerable heel.

The Achillean Flaws

One might take the story of Achilles to mean that destiny is ruled by fate and man has little to do with the ultimate outcome. I believe the myth teaches a different lesson. While Achilles' mortal heel was the *direct* cause of his demise, his truer weakness was expressed in the flaws of character that inevitably led him along the path to destruction. The choices Achilles made in life were rarely noble. Too often he was guided not by the higher purpose of the Trojan War but by his own moods and whims. Achilles' consuming wrath, his unrequited desires, and his inner arrogance were larger than life, greater, it would seem, than those of a mere mortal. They belonged to the character of a demigod, unbalanced by oversized abilities and ambitions. He walked among others as a man, but he was much more. Achilles had the ear of the gods, and because of that he viewed himself as invincible.

The story of Achilles is the story of hubris—the consequences of the nine flaws of disloyalty, greed, hostility, betrayal, withdrawal, inflexibility, deceit, vengeance, and arrogance. These negative qualities were Achilles' real vulnerabilities, and they are actively at work in our current business environment. Although most of us understand intuitively that such qualities do not lead to greatness, we often cannot conceive of doing business any other way. Is it possible to be successful in a competitive, cutthroat atmosphere armed only with such qualities as humility, cooperation, and compassion? Is it possible to reach the top without being ruthless? Can success be attained by doing the right thing? Can invincibility come from honesty and restraint? These are the questions that the legend of Achilles poses for the business world as we prepare to enter the twenty-first century.

In this book we will view the nine flaws of Achilles as they might be experienced in the new age at work. These flaws, which consistently elevate one's personal goals, status, and success above that of the greater good, are devastating to ultimate success. Untamed egos constantly sabotage the mission, demoralize workers, and diminish productivity. The flaws can be objectified as strategic impediments, but they are really moral failings. Our own culture celebrates the most rapacious and predatory, the cruelest and most brutal people, as the real winners. These "stars"—be they in the world of business, sport, or art—represent our culture's heroes. Is someone a hero who does not behave heroically? The amoral and immoral among us have often reaped the greatest material rewards, while their companies and workers paid a devastating price.

These flaws are too often apparent in today's managers and corporate superstars. Even while paying lip service to the ideas of teamwork, empowered employees, job satisfaction, fairness, and rewards for a job well done, these men and women are incapable of following through on such positive goals because they don't really believe in them. What they do believe is that they alone—by virtue of their brilliance, hard work, financial success, status, or ruthlessness—deserve to be set apart, to play by different rules, to consider their own needs first.

The lessons we can derive from the story of Achilles prove to be timeless and perhaps more relevant than ever in today's corporate climate. Intense global competition on every level has made survival as tenuous as it proved to be in the Greek legends. Too often, like Achilles, we grow distracted by the narrow focus of our work and fail to see the larger picture. Our leaders become arrogant and self-indulgent, seduced by the false security of their positions. The common good is neglected in favor of the quest for personal power, wealth, and status. Companies feel little loyalty to their workers, and, in return, workers feel no loyalty to their companies. Desperate to survive, people decide that any means justifies that end.

Downsizing, a concept once heralded as a wise solution to the excesses of American business, has failed to make companies leaner and more effective. Instead, it seems to have created value for the privileged few at the expense of the common good. In recent years, mass firings have become the norm: 40,000 workers at AT&T, 75,000 workers at General Motors, 50,000 workers at Sears, 60,000 workers at IBM, 30,000 workers at Boeing. According to the Department of Labor, between 1993 and 1995 more than 8.4 million people were laid off as the result of corporate mergers or restructuring. That's one out of fourteen workers! And even though most workers have found another job, fully two-thirds have failed to achieve the same pay level or benefits that they enjoyed at their previous job. *Sixty-seven percent of all workers are making less than they did before.*

The megacorporations have become like some mighty Zeus, or Apollo, arbitrarily wielding lightning bolts or sending arrows at unsuspecting workers. Company employees were once secure in the knowledge that if they gave their most productive working years for the good of their companies, they would be rewarded with pensions and benefits. No longer. Instead, older workers are tossed aside with barely a thanks for their contribution. The company to which they pledged their loyalty has become absorbed by some other corporate entity and no longer exists to meet its part of the bargain. Such an uncertain atmosphere predictably creates jealousy, pettiness, deception, greed, and hostility in the workplace. The demons of personal fear intrude on and finally overwhelm the cooperative spirit needed to forge successful operations.

In an era when organizations pay so much attention to technological innovations, too little thought is given to the needs of the human beings in these organizations. Although the pace and magnitude of technological change is dazzling, we sometimes forget that human nature has not altered over the ages. It has always been true that people's attitudes, motives, and behavior are largely influenced by the environment in which they live and work. In light of this, corporations and their managers should be investing the same kind of effort and energy into directing and upgrading the workplace environment as they put into producing profits. You can't have profits without productivity.

Certainly there are exceptions. Some companies provide a myriad of on-site conveniences for their workers, hoping to make everyone's lives easier and less stressful and ultimately hoping, as a by-product, to increase both productivity and civility in the workplace. But there aren't enough visible exceptions to create a momentum for making the producers of the products matter as much as the products themselves.

Protect Your Achilles Heel

The story of Achilles is a story about failing to control the negative forces of human nature. As you will see, there are consequences for this failure. The examples in this book clearly illustrate the ways we share the nine flaws of Achilles and teach how we might manage and overcome them. These lessons are relevant whether you are a corporate CEO, a mid-level manager, the owner of a small company, a team leader on a factory floor, or anyone else who participates in doing work for others. They suggest ways you can begin to construct a different kind of armor for the new age at work—armor crafted of the immortal and timeless truths concerning productivity, success, and satisfaction. Illuminated and followed, these truths can provide a mighty shield, better to fend off the negative forces around you.

Like the legendary Achilles, you too will rise or fall according to your personal strengths and weaknesses and your own destiny. You may possess talents and skills that allow you to be a force for good in both your personal life and your organization. But, like Achilles, you also have vulnerabilities that must be shielded—and for which you must craft the effective armor you need in this new age at work. Your fate lies in your choice. Will it be the poisoned arrow or the shield?

1

DISLOYALTY

Achilles reneges on his sworn oath to join
Agamemnon and the other assembled Greek armies
in the approaching war on Troy

SOON AFTER Achilles promises Agamemnon that he will
fight beside him in the war against Troy, Thetis, his devoted
mother, learns of his intentions. She rises out of the mists
of the sea and appears before Achilles, imploring him not
to go. She knows that Achilles' mortal destiny is fated: He
will be cut down in his prime if he joins the war against
Troy. Her love for him is too strong to allow this passively.
Thetis's powers as a goddess are strong, and she uses them
to induce Achilles to forgo his pledge of allegiance to his
brother Greeks.

She speaks to her son in soft, persuasive tones, reminding him that he is not just a mere mortal and therefore
should not be expected to behave as a mere mortal. She is

a goddess and Achilles is almost a god, and both are beloved of Zeus. How do the oaths of mere mortals apply to such as Achilles, greatest of all Greek warriors? Mortal men make vows to one another that hold them in place, she tells him. Gods are not bound by such limitations; gods make vows that can be spun of impenetrable weave, or of weaves so fine they are as clear as glass. One is heavy, solid, substantial, earthly; the other is weightless, airy, ephemeral, heavenly. Gods choose which vows they keep and which they ignore. Gods decide, and mortals abide.

Achilles believes his mother. He is persuaded by the force of her arguments and by her great love for him. He allows her to convey him to the Isle of Skyros and the court of King Lycomedes, where the great warrior is dressed as one of the king's daughters to prevent his discovery.

Nothing tells us if Achilles tries to persuade his mother that his sense of honor demands he fulfill his promise and lend his formidable talents and skills to the war. We only know that his mother's powers are strong, and he ultimately agrees to go into hiding. It is not exactly the classic definition of heroic behavior, but as a demigod Achilles feels justified in playing by different rules.

Agamemnon is distressed by Achilles' disappearance. He needs Achilles in order to have any chance of success against the Trojans. But beyond that, how does it look to the other leaders of the assembled Greek armies if Agamemnon does not have Achilles and his men at his command? It reveals a breach in Agamemnon's authority before the enterprise has even been undertaken. This cannot be tolerated; it is entirely unacceptable. So Agamemnon orders Ulysses to find Achilles. (Ulysses has also tried to avoid going to war by pretending to be crazy but has already been exposed.)

Once Ulysses finds him, Achilles is quickly convinced to forget his promises to his mother, and in another breach of faith—this time to Thetis—he agrees to join Ulysses and the other Greeks in the siege of Troy. But his clear capacity for faithlessness has been fully established. Achilles may be a great warrior, a demigod, and leader of the Myrmidons, but he has a real problem with loyalty, fidelity, and keeping his word.

A Modern Parable:
Broken Promises, Shattered Trust

This is the story of a very powerful and wealthy man, the owner and CEO of one of the largest privately held companies in America, with holdings in real estate, airlines, oil refineries, and major supermarket chains. His company has assets in excess of $2 billion, and he has a personal net worth of $380 million.

Eight years ago, his company took over a small urban supermarket chain, with twelve stores, promising to revitalize the crumbling enterprise and make it an example of urban renewal and prosperity. This was good news for the neighborhoods, the city, and the workforce. It is well understood that a true sign of urban health is the vitality of local businesses. This man's commitment was particularly heartening, for two of the stores were located in depressed neighborhoods where supermarkets were scarce and jobs were hard to come by.

In a press conference to announce his purchase, the new owner stood beside the beaming mayor and spoke glowingly of his dedication. "I love this city and its people," he said. "I am very pleased that my resources can be used to benefit its future."

A reporter asked, "Will there be layoffs?" and he replied, "I'm not in this business to put people out of work." Later, the newspapers applauded the fact that a man of such personal and corporate wealth and prestige would invest in the city, rather than abandoning it as so many others had done.

Within months of the takeover, however, the tune was changing. Two weeks before Christmas, an announcement came from "management" stating that three stores would be closed the following year and 15 percent of the workers would be laid off. In an attempt to put a positive spin on the decision, the owner was quoted as saying, "I regret the necessity of this action. I can only assure you that it is in the interest of making all the stores profitable. There will be no further closings or layoffs. We are more committed than ever to the success of this venture and our investment in the city."

The event barely made a ripple in the city at large. Fewer

than 75 workers were laid off; the three stores had been located in blighted neighborhoods. But those who lost their jobs felt abandoned without explanation, and those who worked in the remaining stores felt a new vulnerability—an unease that never quite subsided. They knew now that in spite of his high-minded words, their new owner had no real commitment to them. In return, they no longer felt committed to him or to his stores. In the end, his faithlessness netted him a huge loss in employee devotion, morale, and productivity.

Lesson One

The Shield of Commitment

When people depend on you for leadership, support, and their very survival, there is no greater blow than the discovery that you are faithless—loyal only when it suits your personal balance sheet. Human beings are not naturally cynical; they want to believe in an essential code of decency that assumes a mutual trust between employers and employees. But more and more, that trust is being frayed. There was a time, as many of us remember fondly, when companies prided themselves on their loyalty to their employees—a loyalty that was returned to them by the workforce. IBM is a good example: The company cultivated an atmosphere of caring, a sense of family. Before 1980, IBM's greatest source of pride was the guarantee of job security. Workers were often reminded that if you worked for IBM your job was safe. Today, there have been tens of thousands of layoffs at IBM, with more to come. IBM might call this effective management, not disloyalty. It didn't seem to trouble chairman and CEO Louis V. Gerstner one bit to collect his $4.8 million salary last year, along with a $2.6 million bonus for a job well done.

It would, of course, be simplistic to say that downsizing, restructuring, and corporate mergers are in themselves acts of disloyalty. But in too many cases, what the workers see is a few higher-ups winning a lottery of huge salaries and bonuses even as they "economize" by cutting the jobs of simple wage earners. This sends a terrible message. How can people trust that your intentions are decent and loyal when you seem to be benefiting so handsomely from taking their jobs away?

Perhaps just as demoralizing as the splurge of corporate downsizing is the way corporations try to mask their true intentions with comforting terms meant to describe massive layoffs. Is it easier for workers to stomach pink slips when they're couched in phases like "career-transition program" (General Motors), "normal payroll adjustment" (Wal-Mart), "strengthening global effectiveness" (Procter & Gamble), or "career change opportunity" (Clifford of Vermont)? Not likely. But it probably makes it easier for the company to put a good face on its actions and to distance itself from the reality of the lives that are being affected.

The aura of distrust, fear, backstabbing, and suspicion that accompanies the sense that no one can be trusted pervades every level. People become obsessed with placing blame when there are mistakes, stealing credit from others, sabotaging their colleagues, and sending out résumés on company time. Paranoia is rampant.

The new age at work requires that you lay a foundation of trust if you want a workforce that is consistently productive. It's the way you prevent your best workers from being lured away from you, the way you inspire goodwill among your employees, the way you eliminate the distractions that fear and suspicion are bound to cause, the way you develop a team that cares about producing value every day. It's simple common sense.

The shield of commitment is your first piece of armor. It is crafted from the following:

❖ BE TRUE TO A CORE IDEOLOGY

Disloyalty was easy for Achilles because he never possessed a deep commitment to Agamemnon's mission in the first place. If your company or division does not have a clearly identified ideology—not just on paper, but in reality—it becomes easy to break commitments. Your core ideology is what protects you from the shifting winds of change. A recent study by two highly accredited business historians going back to 1925 shows that companies that have adhered to a core ideology have dramatically outperformed the general stock market.

What is a core ideology? It's a foundation that remains consistent no matter what happens. It's timeless—as relevant a hundred years ago as it is today. It answers the question, "Why are we here?" It serves as a talisman in times of change.

Core ideologies are by their nature an expression of human values—the principles you would teach your children, the beliefs you hold yourself. A values-driven workplace inspires trust and devotion.

❀ BE DECISIVE

As an effective manager, you're the one who always remains stalwart, in good times and bad. People know they can count on you—that you won't break contracts, disassociate yourself from unpopular decisions, or leave them in the lurch to do impossible jobs. You may not be in a position to control the axes that fall from above where the big bosses sit, but the people who report directly to you know you will do your best to shield them from disaster—and they, in turn, will shield you.

In today's uncertain business climate of downsizing, it's all too easy to cut and run when it's a question of you or them. If you can't make a decision without waiting to see which way the wind is blowing, or which course of action will benefit *you* the most, you cannot be an effective leader. Indecision and fear are crippling qualities.

A relevant example is the communications manager whose job it was to write her boss's marketing reports for shareholder meetings. She was the fifth person to hold the job in less than three years—and no wonder. Her boss would provide a few facts and very little input, then wait for her to produce a brilliant document. Soon after she presented him with a draft of her report, it would appear back in her in-basket with scrawled comments like "No!" or "Not right" or "Say this another way." His input was so vague she would go to his office to ask for more details. His response would be extreme annoyance. "I'm very busy," he'd say sharply. "If you can't figure it out, maybe you're in the wrong job." The communications manager would leave the office at the end of the day, her stomach churning. She was always on the verge of being fired.

People cannot work effectively when they live in a state of unease and suspicion. If as a manager you behave in arbitrary ways, change your mind frequently, and blame others for your mistakes, your workers will not trust you. If you don't keep your promises, if you're abusive, or if you fire people without warning, your working environment will reflect that. No organization can prosper under these conditions. Workers will not be loyal to a company that is not loyal to them.

❧ *STAY LOYAL TO YOUR PEOPLE*

Sometimes things go wrong or unexpected events un-ravel a company's carefully laid plans. That doesn't mean you're justified in throwing up your hands and declaring that all promises are off. Whether you're the owner of the company or the manager of a division, you are by definition responsible for the well-being of those who work for you.

A remarkable example of a business owner who showed loyalty and commitment to his workers in dire circum-stances is Aaron Feuerstein, who owns a textile mill in Me-thuen, Massachusetts. On December 11, 1995, the mill was destroyed in an all-consuming fire. As Feuerstein's 2,400 employees tried to comprehend the horror of finding themselves suddenly out of work two weeks before Christ-mas, Feuerstein made an announcement. He would rebuild the mill. And while it was being rebuilt, he would continue paying his workers. Everyone was stunned. So rarely does a business owner behave in such an exemplary and gra-cious manner, Feuerstein's action received a huge play in the media. Newspaper, magazine, radio, and television re-porters besieged him, eager for interviews.

❁ *FOCUS ON YOUR JOB,*
  NOT ON SAVING YOUR SKIN

Truly successful managers look ahead, not behind. You are creative, courageous, and noble. You stand apart from the crowd. You have vision. These are not merely empty words. They define the essence of leadership. If you lack these qualities or the drive to achieve them, you shouldn't be a manager.

Leadership also requires that you be the first to make sacrifices during tough times. Fly in the face of precedent and take a cut yourself before you demand that your employees make any grave sacrifices. Can you imagine the reaction if an executive whose salary already ranged in the millions decided to use that extra two mil bonus to keep a number of valuable workers employed? Sure, Wall Street might grumble (it doesn't like high employment), but the returns you would realize in employee commitment might be worth it.

❁ *DON'T TOLERATE THE BLAME*
  GAME FROM EMPLOYEES

Make it absolutely clear through your words and actions that you have no tolerance for employees who turn on their colleagues. If a worker comes to you during a crisis and tries to convince you that he had nothing to do with it but Joe next door did, cut him off in midsentence. An effective manager understands that employees must be loyal to one another in order to operate as a unified team. Back-stabbing drags everyone down. At the same time, try to find out on your own if Joe next door *did* create the crisis, and then concentrate on solving the problem.

❀ *IF YOU MUST BREAK A COMMITMENT, DO IT HONORABLY*

There are times, within every business, when it becomes necessary to cut your losses and change course. Do it honorably. That means treating the other parties with respect, doing everything you can to repair the damage, and not leaving others feeling as though they've simply been dumped. Those who behave honorably in their transactions, especially during difficult times, are repaid with the respect and confidence of others.

Here's a chilling example of complete indifference and a lack of commitment to the people who work for you. Albert Dunlap, whose nickname is "Chainsaw Al," is proud of his reputation for being able to parachute into troubled companies and, like a chainsaw, tear ruthlessly through the infrastructure, slashing costs, selling assets, and laying off workers without a moment of regret or thought for the cost to human lives. In the process, Dunlap makes fortunes for himself. One recent coup, an eighteen-month stint at Sunbeam Corporation, netted him $100 million and made a lot of money for shareholders, but the process was extremely ugly. Chainsaw Al doesn't care. His dedication is to profit. Recently, he wrote a braggart's tale, titled *Mean Business: How I Save Bad Companies and Make Good Companies Great* (Times Books, 1996). Dunlap needs a reality check. "Mean" and "great" can't exist in the same company.

When faced with a choice between keeping his vow to join Agamemnon and the other Greeks in the siege of Troy or looking after himself, Achilles chose himself. Whether motivated by fear, pragmatism, or simply deference to his mother, his decision could only weaken the great warrior in the eyes of the Greeks. It established him forever as someone who was capable of turning his back on those who depended on him. His obsession was with his own importance. He believed he was irreplaceable, so his own safety took priority over the lives of thousands of others. Achilles' flaw of disloyalty—manifested as loyalty to self alone—would present itself again and again, for disloyalty is never a one-time thing.

2

GREED

To the victor belongs the spoils:
The Greek leaders divide the riches of war

AGAMEMNON AND ACHILLES are participants in a culture whose leaders expect and receive spectacular tribute. Sometimes that ritual of excessive reward turns to greed, thus undermining the success of the mission. Even in the mythical world of the *Iliad,* where ethics and honor are structured by godly whim, a bitter price can be paid for greed.

When Achilles joins the war against the Trojans, he takes his place as the leader of the Myrmidons, his own army. Though Achilles is acknowledged as the greatest of the warriors, he submits to the authority of Agamemnon, the chosen commander in chief of the assembled Greek armies.

Although they have been unsuccessful against Troy for nine arduous years, the Greeks are able to sweep through the many neighboring and allied cities surrounding Troy, raiding and plundering them of food, riches, and women.

After one such raid, Agamemnon and Achilles acquire two beautiful maidens, Chryseis and Briseis. Slavery and concubinage are common—to the victor belongs the spoils, even if those spoils are human.

Agamemnon's prize, the beautiful Chryseis, is a maiden of great stature, the daughter of Chryses, a priest of Apollo. Briseis, meanwhile, quickly captures Achilles' heart with her warmth, grace, and beauty.

The god Apollo's priest, Chryses, is tormented by the loss of his daughter. Though weakened by age, he makes his way to the tent of Agamemnon and humbly begs the great king for the return of his sweet young daughter. Not only does the priest bear the supplicant staff of the god Apollo, he also offers a very rich ransom. But Agamemnon is in no rush to return Chryseis, whom he finds very comforting. He coldly refuses the priest's entreaties and has the old man driven from his camp.

In deep despair, Chryses appeals to Apollo for justice and intercession, and Apollo, angered by Agamemnon's cruelty and disrespect, strings his silver bow and comes down from Olympus in a killing rage. He begins to fire arrow after arrow at the Greeks and so visits a great plague upon them, a killing plague. Hundreds and hundreds of men die because of King Agamemnon's appetite for the daughter of Apollo's priest. Funeral pyres darken the sky above the Greek camps.

Achilles busies himself in his tent, waiting for a resolution to the crisis, not knowing that its cause rests in the audacious behavior of Agamemnon. The remains of the Greek forces huddle around their fires. They also wait— wondering why the gods hold them in such disfavor.

A Modern Parable: The Plagues of Man's Greed

Crown Industries was a strong and healthy company, having carved a very nice niche for itself in the automotive components industry. Crown had been in business for over sixty years, and many of the workers lived in the surrounding community. Crown and the small city in which it operated grew up together—comfortable, if not prosperous. There was a sense of security in the city that was very rare indeed in these fast-changing times. Recently, the trend in outsourcing for components had given Crown a brand new burst of profitability.

Then, like a bolt out of the blue, Crown was targeted by a group specializing in corporate takeovers. Run by un-principled pirates of unimaginable wealth, this was like a game for them. The management of Crown was baffled. Why would *their* company be targeted? Weren't corporate takeovers reserved for companies that were failing? That was certainly not the case with Crown. Nobody could explain it to the dazed and enriched shareholders, all of whom found themselves new stockholders in some huge rollover entity. The board of directors, the management, and the workers were all unable to stop the acquisition. It was as though a giant had strolled across their landscape and simply swept the company up because it was in its path. Nor could anyone understand why, just one year after the takeover, the formerly sound company was a hollow shell of its former self. Why would an enormous corporation go out of its way to take over a company if they didn't want to make a profit from it?

Of course, they *had* made a profit. Everyone else was behind the curve. The basic strategy had changed. The corporate takeover gods were not targeting companies that were failing, companies which they could reorder, strengthen, and improve. The new strategy was to target companies that were healthy but had undervalued assets.

Once the takeover was secured, the new owners would simply divide and conquer, selling off assets, decimating the company's foundation. These takeover artists weren't interested in building strong companies. They were interested in emptying their acquisitions of all value, reaching maximum profit potential, and then dumping the shell back onto the market, selling what was left cheaply. In the process, they reaped unimaginable rewards for themselves and their clients.

In the case of Crown Industries, more than a company was lost. Although the new owners had initially assured both management and labor that they had every intention of making the company better than ever, it soon became clear what *better* really meant. Within thirty days of the initial takeover, an entirely new management team was brought in by the new parent company to reorder the corporate culture. The labor force was reduced by almost half within sixty days, and within the year Crown Industries, its workers, and the surrounding communities found themselves in an economic tailspin. Every profitable division of Crown was sold within a year of the takeover, and the company itself changed hands once again within eighteen months of the original deal. Crown is now a special products division of the giant P. J. Delmar Corporation and employs only 20 percent of its previous workforce. The entire region has experienced a downturn since the corporate privateers came sailing through their world.

When people asked, "Why did they do this?" the answer was clear: They did it because they could. They thought they deserved to reap the spoils of their brilliant gamesmanship, with no concern for how many lives might be ruined in the process. They were following the ancient code: To the victor belongs the spoils.

Lesson Two

The Shield of Selflessness

Today it is the great corporate leaders who seem to see no relationship between the rewards they receive and the suffering they cause. The examples are plentiful. Recently, AT&T CEO Robert Allen captured national headlines when he announced that 40,000 jobs would be cut in his company—a cost-paring strategy for which he personally was richly rewarded with a huge salary increase and bonus and added stock options. The AT&T layoffs drew cheers from Wall Street, but they created quite a stir in the media. The imbalance was so crystal clear that finally (maybe because it was an election year) people started to ask why the layoffs were necessary in the first place. AT&T was a healthy company by every measure. It used to be that layoffs were a grim necessity for companies on the brink of disaster. How could the blow to 40,000 lives be explained? How could Allen's phenomenal payback be justified? The smooth-talking economists had answers, but they didn't ring true to the people who lost their jobs. To them, it seemed like a piggish strategy: nothing more than greed.

Another example of "take the money and run" was Steve Ross, the corporate genius of Warner Communications, who achieved synergy with Time-Life in a then-enormous merger in 1989, a few years before he died. Somewhere in the wheeling and dealing, Ross managed to pocket well over

$100 million from the deal alone and much, much more in terms of perks and options. But for some mysterious reason, the new Time Warner megacompany was saddled with an enormous mountain of ballooning debt that threatened to destroy the merger in its first few years of operation. That 1989 merger is easily dwarfed by the 1996 merger that will further morph Time Warner's operations with those of other megacorporations controlled by Ted Turner, John Malone, and Edgar Bronfman.

The recent Bell Atlantic–NYNEX merger hasn't produced personal payoffs in the multimillion-dollar range. Still, a handful of top executives in each company are getting seven-figure bonuses, while in the lower echelons people wait for the ax to fall. At least 3,000 employees will be eliminated right away, and few people doubt there will be more to follow.

The first years of the 1990s have seen more megamergers than at any time before or since Ronald Reagan's demonopolization of the early 1980s. Recently, four major American television networks have been purchased by larger entities: Disney now owns ABC, Westinghouse owns CBS, General Electric owns NBC, and the Australian tycoon Rupert Murdoch's News Corporation owns the Fox Network.

Everything is moving so fast and so many deals are being made that even disgrace and imprisonment aren't what they used to be. The formerly disgraced Michael Milken of junk-bond fame has been paid $50 million for brokering a deal in the merger between Time Warner, Turner, et al. And that's only a fraction of what the resurrected Milken has earned from companies since he served his jail sentence. All is easily forgiven when there's big money to be made.

This is not an indictment of all the movers and shakers in the business world. Not everyone who deals in big money is motivated by greed. Some new companies, such as Dreamworks SKG, are formed to allow talented tycoons to work with other like-minded tycoons. Within the fairly narrow world of the entertainment industry, there is certainly a lot of talent moving from corporation to corporation, a lot of alliances being reshaped and reformed. But too often these arrangements appear to fit the definition of corporate greed—a few people realizing phenomenal personal wealth at the expense of the many. In fact, the underlying principle of greed—a focus on what you personally can reap from every venture—has become an acceptable motivational business strategy. It's not called greed, of course. It's called "just dues" or "tribute" or "what you deserve." But it amounts to the same thing. In the long run, leaders more concerned with reaping the spoils of success than with the long-term welfare of the company achieve a pyrrhic victory. If their company and its workers don't prosper, if their leaders' actions leave behind the ruins of unemployment, closed factories, and regional recession, it's hard to view such behavior as a blueprint for success.

The new age at work requires leaders of companies to create a corporate culture that becomes less self-indulgent and more selfless. That's not simply an altruistic notion, it's highly pragmatic. Every company is so dependent on the success or failure of others that the ancient rules of competition no longer apply. Is it good business practice to destroy yourself in the process of destroying the competition? Are business decisions being made today going to produce long-term growth and prosperity, or will the impetus fizzle with time?

Greed is a destructive force within companies as well. It destroys the spirit of cooperation. Greed inspires anger and resentment and, for the few who find that money comes easily to them, breeds cynicism and an air of entitlement. For those fighting against waves of greed, the shield of selflessness is the second piece of armor, crafted from the following:

❂ *SHARE THE REWARDS*

In every company, there are a few stars supported by a vast network of workers, who form the anonymous backbone that makes everything happen. When hardworking people in a company feel they don't get proper recognition or reward for their contributions, the result is a decline in morale, enthusiasm, and productivity. If a business is doing well, the employees should be rewarded by bonuses provided by management, as well as by improved wages, working conditions, and whatever perks the company sees fit to provide. On-site shopping, banking, medical services, pharmacy, day care, dry cleaning, exercise facilities, food courts, and flex time are some of the ways companies try to share the rewards of their success by making their employees' lives easier and less stressful. These companies recognize the simple truth that when the workers are satisfied, they perform better—and so does the company.

❖ DON'T GET GREEDY

If you're an up-and-comer in your company, the lure of great rewards can be dazzling—so seductive that you are blinded by its light. If you're a smart, competitive, aggressive person eagerly climbing the ladder to success, tread carefully as you reach the middle rungs. Stop for a moment and examine your position. Where have you come from and where are you going? What really matters to you? It seems easy to be seduced by success, to have your moral compass shaken by good fortune. In the rarefied atmosphere of the important and successful, it's possible to adopt a warped vision of reality. What you would normally have seen as greed now seems merely to be what you deserve. Corrupt practices and policies that benefit you, in the clearer light of success, now seem like shrewd gamesmanship. It's just the way things are done; the naysayers are just envious. Like the Gordon Gekko character in Oliver Stone's popular movie *Wall Street* says, with utter conviction, "Greed is good."

Joseph Jett is a sad example of a man who got sucked into the abyss of greed. When Jett was appointed chief of government trading by Kidder, Peabody & Company in 1993, there was nothing particularly remarkable about him. In fact, he'd been fired for poor performance by two previous companies. Many people thought he was the wrong man for the job. Jett decided to show them differently. Within a year, as his portfolio grew to $18 billion, he was being heralded as a genius. In his first year, he earned a $9-million bonus. The glory didn't last long. It was discovered that Jett had faked $350 million in trades to cover losses of $100 million. Most people blamed Jett for this terrible fraud, but a few also pointed accusing fingers at the culture of a company whose own greed was so deeply entrenched it failed to detect the fraud sooner.

Is it possible to become highly successful and not lose your way? Can you keep your conscience when you're reaping vast rewards? The answer is, only if you balance yourself on the ladder, keep focused on who you are and where you're going, and maintain a core of humility—reminding yourself of how fleeting are the treasures of mortal men.

❀ NEVER TAKE WHAT RIGHTFULLY BELONGS TO OTHERS

Rewards gained by less than fair play are not worth the price of your honor. Never take what belongs to others, be it their money, their belongings, their reputation, or their credit for having done something you think so admirable that you would claim it as your own. Whether the theft is practical, spiritual, or intellectual, it is theft, and you are diminished by that behavior.

Intellectual property theft is a constant in companies and is obviously very tempting for executives and managers. Asked to put together a concept, write a report, or solve a problem, the executive delegates his subordinates to handle it for him. And, of course, they do. If the team works well and produces an exceptional effort, accolades are showered on the executive from above. Not on his subordinates, not on his team; it is the executive who receives the bonus, the raise, and the promotion. The members of his team hope to be remembered as useful to him and be elevated along with him to his new position. But those who do the brunt of the real work and receive no recognition can only feel cheated.

A good manager will always make sure to give credit where it's due: "Mary's team made a fine effort on this report"; "Everyone put in extra time"; "It was Jim's idea to solve the problem this way." If the higher-ups in your company shower you with rewards for efforts generated by your team, make sure your people get their share—whether it comes from above or from you. And be generous about recommending deserving workers for promotions, even if that means losing their services yourself.

❧ PROMOTE SOCIAL RESPONSIBILITY

Several prosperous companies—among them American Express, IBM, and Xerox, offer paid social-service leaves to their employees because they've discovered that charitable service to the community makes workers happier and reflects well on the company. Participating employees normally take a three- to six-month leave and use their skills to help organizations that are performing charitable work in the United States and abroad. These programs, now operative in only 5 percent of Fortune 500 companies, may become increasingly popular as workers search for meaning in their lives and satisfaction beyond the paycheck.

❧ MAKE SACRIFICES AT THE TOP

It stands to reason that those who reap the rewards in good times should be called upon to make sacrifices when times are hard. But when was the last time you heard of a company bigwig taking a pay cut or refusing a bonus to demonstrate solidarity with the workers? Making sacrifices for the good of the company usually seems to fall on the shoulders of those whose salaries are inconsequential compared with the responsibilities heaped upon them. Sacrifice seems reserved for the new hires, the most junior associate, the person least able to demur.

But here we are talking about perception as well as reality. If the people who work for you know that you are absolutely fair with them in the wages paid, that your attitude toward them is reasonable, and every opportunity is given to make sure that the workload is equally distributed, very few employees are going to have a complaint. Certainly most company owners—especially when the company is privately held—seem to take home a disproportionately large percentage of income compared to their workers. However, the risks and responsibilities of ownership often require countless hardships and sacrifices for the good of the company that employees may never even know about. The worker, meanwhile, goes home when the shift is over and doesn't share these headaches or risks.

Showing your workers that sacrifices start at the top can be a symbolic but very important gesture. When Jack Smith became president and CEO of General Motors, he declined to work in the cushy, well-guarded suite of offices that had separated his predecessors from the masses. Not only did he think it sent the terrible message of *us* versus *them* down the ranks of his company, he felt it was too costly and it isolated him from the real workings of the company. He abandoned the lofty tower in Detroit and moved his office to the GM Technical Center in Warren,

Michigan. It was a powerful symbol of Smith's message that he was not above the workers; he was one of them.

In the ancient world of the *Iliad,* the culture in which Achilles and Agamemnon lived remained firm while the fate of man was misshapen by godly whim. Greed almost seemed like a tool wielded by the gods to drive men mad, to undo the clasps of reason and decency, to rip away the last shreds of reasonable and decent behavior—and then, finally, to rain down punishment.

The spoils of war taunted and tempted men who were drunk with their own power and achievement, even as they do today. But there is always a price to pay.

3

HOSTILITY

*Agamemnon and Achilles face off
in a scathing power struggle that changes
the course of the Trojan War*

THE PLAGUE CONTINUES. Each day brings new deaths and
more funeral pyres. The air soon becomes thick with black
smoke and the sweet fetid odor of burning flesh. Still Achilles waits, patiently deferring to the rule of Agamemnon.
But on the tenth day of black smoke and burning flesh,
Achilles erupts. Someone must take charge, someone must
take action. Someone must lead. Sending heralds, Achilles
calls for an assembly of all the Greeks and then demands
answers. He wants the cause of this pestilence and death
to be identified and dealt with.

Calchas the soothsayer rises out of the assembled masses.
He is a seer, and he knows why the god Apollo is angry,
but he tells Achilles that he is afraid to speak for fear of what
might befall him.

Achilles readily promises Calchas that he will be safe, even if he names Achilles himself as the cause of the Greek armies' troubles.

Thus reassured, Calchas exposes Agamemnon as the reason for the plague. He reveals that the maiden Chryseis's father is a priest of Apollo, the god of the deadly silver bow. When the priest's pleas for his daughter's safe return were rudely rebuffed by Agamemnon, Apollo heard his imprecations and came down from the heights of Olympus furious, unleashing the arrows of pestilence and plague upon the Greeks.

Achilles is stunned when he finally understands the cause of so many of his allies' deaths. He confronts Agamemnon before the assembled Greeks and demands that he return the priest's daughter without recompense. "Give this girl to the god," Achilles demands, "and if ever Zeus grant us to sack the city of Troy we will requite you three and fourfold." The offer to requite Agamemnon three and fourfold is sneered by Achilles as an insult, and it is received as one. There are shouts of derision from among the troops. They see this quarrel between Achilles and Agamemnon as long coming. Achilles is known to bear the brunt of the fighting, while Agamemnon has become famous for his hesitations and excuses. Agamemnon is always the first to choose which spoils he wants before any are offered elsewhere. He is greedy and spoiled and lets others do the fighting for him. Achilles, on the other hand, is a master warrior, feared and ferocious, respected by both Greeks and

Trojans for his prowess with sword, lance, spear, and shield.

Agamemnon is infuriated and humiliated by Achilles' reproach. He feels cornered. There is no way out of this confrontation without some profound loss of face. As king and commander in chief, he cannot allow that to occur.

The strategy in this situation is ancient and clear: Whoever attacks the leader must be attacked in return. Everyone is watching; everyone is waiting: Achilles against Agamemnon. You can hear the murmurs, men turning to one another and making small wagers on who'll draw first blood, on who will die.

As though the entire assembly has exhaled as one, Agamemnon turns and attacks Achilles. The attack is not physical; Agamemnon knows he stands no chance against this warrior. The attack is on Achilles' ego, position, and possessions. In a ringing voice, Agamemnon announces that Chryseis will be returned to her father. However, he adds, he must be compensated for this loss. He declares that his compensation will be the acquisition of Briseis, Achilles' war prize and beloved.

Now the Furies dance on Olympus. A huge wind begins to roar out of sudden calm. Agamemnon has struck hard at Achilles, and the wound to his pride creates a vast rent. Surely he, the greatest warrior of all the Greeks, should not have to take such insults, especially from a man such as Agamemnon, and certainly not in front of the assembled Greeks.

Rage and hatred build a hot fire. Achilles' honor has been

challenged. Instantly this is uppermost in his mind—not the Trojan War, not the welfare of his men, not even the threatened loss of Briseis.

Achilles rebukes Agamemnon for his boldness and challenges him before the assembly. The insults and threats between the two leaders quickly escalate, and neither will back down. Too much is at stake.

With one further threat from Agamemnon, Achilles begins to draw his sword. The swift intervention of Athena, goddess of wisdom, stays Achilles' hand. But the glint of metal, the familiar movement of Achilles' arm, has raised a roar of anticipation in the crowd. The roar dies to a groan of disappointment. It is clear to the troops that, had the goddess not intervened, Agamemnon's head would have been severed from his neck in a swift flash of metal.

The crowd quiets. Achilles turns and faces them, his face a terrible mask of wrath. In a loud voice that singes the air with bitterness and anger, he vows on his royal scepter that he and his troops will withdraw from the war and return home. He warns that one day

"You shall look fondly for Achilles and not find him.
In the day of your distress, when your men fall dying . . .
you shall rend your heart with rage for the hour
when you offered insult to the bravest of the Greeks."

And then he storms away.

A Modern Parable:
Cultures Clashing, Giant Egos Warring

No one believed they were going to be able to slip this one by the feds, and when they finally did they were jubilant. This was the megamerger of megamergers, the Rosetta Stone of deals! Four massive corporations, each with a brilliant and powerful leader, were collectively creating a communications conglomerate that would dominate all important media. The industry was *theirs!*

Now, there was a real problem. There were too many *theirs* in this deal, too many big players. Each came with his own company, his own rules, his own way of doing things, his own people. A giant clash of egos, as dramatic as the ancient wars, was inevitable. Who was going to rule this priceless kingdom?

Of course, these savvy businessmen and their troops of lawyers had already signed agreements that laid out all the details. Every *t* had been crossed, every *i* dotted. But these were words on paper, not beings who lived, breathed, and plotted. The real war for control of this new corporate behemoth would occur in the day-to-day operations. Which corporate culture would prevail?

One of the principals (we'll call him Principal A) had always run an operation that was famous for its low overhead. He believed in a team-oriented approach that stressed deference to the boss (him), while diminishing the impact of the star players on the team. In this way lines of authority and responsibility remained clear, and all decision making filtered up to Principal A and his number-two man. But he had just merged with a giant company, run by Principal B, that had a completely different operation. Principal B's company had many powerful and acknowledged leaders. Each division had its own president, vice president, and assistant vice president, all with their attendant courts of executive assistants, administrative assistants, and assistants to the assistants, all of *them* with the requisite offices and secretarial support. While only four executives in Principal A's entire company made a salary in excess of one million dollars, over forty executives in Principal B's company enjoyed such compensation. How long would that be allowed to continue?

Within six months of this merger, Principal A had climbed to the top of the corporate mountaintop and planted his flag. He just happened to plant that flag in the prone body of Principal B, his former ally. The "mountain" was composed of the heaped bodies of former employees and divisions of Principal B's megacorporation that had been dumped in a clean sweep of corporate excess and job duplication, leaving a new lean-and-mean corporate culture that would see clear profit within ten months of the merger.

And what of the other partners, Principal C and Principal D? They remained on the sidelines for the time being, constrained by sweeping federal regulations that limited their input and control. But they watched with great interest as Principal A cut a swath through the corporate fat of their mutually owned giant, able only through indirect influence to make their wishes and desires known. Within months they would find themselves facing an unexpected buyout bid from Principal A, in his attempt to force their companies also to adopt his corporate culture of extreme downsizing, including divisional and executive elimination. Principal A made it clear that he was now the Captain of this massive ship, and they would sail at his pleasure.

You can imagine the reactions of Principal A's fellow magnates as the truth hit home. It seems that Principal A had merely used them as stepping stones to his own ascension. Clearly, his intention had always been to take the wheel of this corporate ship and sail it into his port, and they were determined to stop him.

Oh, to understand the Byzantine intricacies of this far-reaching deal, to understand the machinations that allowed all the disparate players to come together and then instantly begin to rip apart the very moorings of their collaboration! As the insults and power-grabbing maneuvers continue, the scene looks much like a modern version of the hostilities that raged between Achilles and Agamemnon. The issue is no longer about work, it is about domination—an obsession with power. True, each principal already enjoys substantial power, but each wants the power of the others to make himself even stronger. Together they control almost everything, but which player will control the most? Who will stand tallest as Leader of the leaders?

The reasoned answer would be that the dust must settle over the trampled plains of this complex deal before anyone will be able to see who and what is left standing. Already the corporate shifting has begun, as longtime sidekicks of the principal players are either eliminated or resign in a huff—bailing out with lush parachutes that will prevent their bespoke suits from getting rumpled. Other longtime loyalists of the principals are placed in bright and powerful new perches, ready to serve their different "masters" in the fight for control. It's such a riveting, larger-than-life confrontation that most people have already forgotten the reasons why this deal was a good idea in the first place.

Lesson Three

The Shield of Cooperation

Somehow it has been established in our current business culture that those who value cooperation and consensus above cutthroat one-upmanship are weak and ineffective—even when the battles are with their own teams. On the face of it, this seems absurd. Why would colleagues who are engaged in a common quest direct their hostilities inward, rather than summoning their combined strength to rise above the competition?

Internal competition is more prevalent in organizations today than ever before. Rather than focusing as a team on external goals, employees are feverishly trying to get an edge over their own colleagues. Intramural warfare is the clear path to failure. We know, for example, that a sports team only succeeds through teamwork. We understand the dire consequences of an army without discipline. The same holds true for companies.

Furthermore, it's clear that quarrels don't resolve disputes any better today than they did in ancient Greece. And humiliating your superior is a foolish way to express a grievance. When you are caught up in quarrels, you lose your focus, turn inward. Your vision is clouded by negativity. You're unable to solve problems wisely. Quarrels and humiliation are the ugly products of the negative forces of human nature. Yet they continue.

Today, it is not unusual to read about executives who resign in disagreement over management style or the future direction of a company. And it is safe to assume that such leave-takings are usually preceded by a severe quarrel with superiors. Most conflicts do not reach the level of media circus. But they are every bit as destructive to the lives involved.

A hostile approach to external competition is likewise crippling. Being competitive is one thing; killing the competition is another. As far as Marc Andreessen, the senior vice president of technology at Netscape Communications Corporation and the man who invented the Internet browser, is concerned, his competitor, Microsoft, "is a bit like the Mafia." He adds, "It's certainly possible to compete without trying to kill."

From the moment Netscape introduced the Internet

browser, which was solely responsible for opening up the Internet to the masses, Microsoft's Bill Gates has been lobbing hand grenades. At first, he called Andreessen's invention "trivial"—which sounded like a case of sour grapes. But things have grown increasingly nasty, and Microsoft is powerful enough to do a lot of damage to Netscape and perhaps destroy it altogether—just as it did with Apple. Gates clearly believes there is only room for one genius and one leader in the entire industry.

But Gates better watch his back. Microsoft Corporation is currently under investigation by the Justice Department for a practice called "technology lock-in." Microsoft's strategy has been to add functions to its operating systems that force customers to buy only its systems. Software manufactured by other companies won't fit. Other computer companies have accused Microsoft of being anticompetitive—of violating policies of fair business practices by trying to own the entire market. These accusations are so widespread that the government has stepped in to study the matter. Microsoft's practices may eventually hurt Gates more than it hurts his competitors.

The new age at work requires cooperation, internally and externally. It may be the single most important factor in securing long-term success. Many companies have already established cooperative endeavors with their competitors. Most visible and most successful of these have been the joint ventures pursued by major automakers. These agreements have made everyone winners. Now the aircraft industry is getting into the act, with a giant joint venture between Rockwell International and Lockheed to build spacecraft for NASA.

Internally, cooperation among workers and between divisions must be carefully encouraged. Although many companies now pay lip service to concepts like productivity teams and employee empowerment and send managers to seminars that motivate them to create a spirit of cooperation in their companies, true cooperation must be developed by example, not mandated. As a manager, you must wear the shield of cooperation. It is your third piece of armor, crafted from the following:

❖ BECOME A CONSENSUS BUILDER

A consensus builder solves problems and negotiates solutions that save face for everyone. It's not an easy skill to master, because there are always going to be situations where the conflicting sides seem absolutely intractable. One key is respecting the fact that each side has a valid point. Objectify the issues beyond emotion.

Another important tool is critical perspective. If your attitude is "We're at war because we've always been at war," you're not going to make progress. The question is, Why are you at war *now?* And what solutions are available?

Chrysler Corporation's change in the way it operated with its suppliers is a great example of breaking dysfunctional business patterns. Historically, the American automotive giants controlled suppliers with ruthless bidding wars and margin squeezing that left everyone—even the winners—feeling unfairly treated. This treatment was the automakers' way of keeping prices down. Since the Big Three—GM, Ford, and Chrysler—mostly shared the same suppliers, there was little room for the suppliers to maneuver in their quest for better treatment. Then Chrysler came up with another idea: Perhaps the system would work better if it were not so adversarial. During the 1990s, Chrysler developed programs that essentially made outside suppliers part of the team. Its most radical development was a program called SCORE: supplier cost reduction effort. Instead of squeezing the margins on supplier profits, Chrysler challenged suppliers to come up with cost-cutting ideas. The idea worked. Suppliers save money, and the automaker gets cheaper parts. Everyone prospers, and the mood of cooperation makes people more satisfied with the current environment than the wars of old.

❁ SETTLE YOUR GRIEVANCES IN PRIVATE

We expect responsible, mature adults to air their hostilities away from public view, but many corporate wars are waged openly—with the public playing the role of excited fans rooting for one side over the other. In these public battles, the winner is often considered a hero, while the loser (or the person who refuses to get engaged in public fights in the first place) is scorned as weak, wishy-washy, cowardly, or a poor leader.

Ross Perot is a master of the public put-down. As Perot himself might say in his colorful style, "Don't leave a snake in the grass if you ain't willin' to get bit." Perot has had a long and some would say distinguished career as a corporate warrior. He can't understand why people don't just see that he knows how to do things right and let him do them. When the world doesn't cooperate, he gets out his big guns. The famous 1980 EDS incident is classic. EDS (Electronic Data Systems) was Perot's major claim to fame, the company that made him a billionaire. The company initially prospered by developing computer programs that processed claims for Medicaid and Medicare, massive government enterprises. EDS went on to practically lock up the insurance business across the country. But in 1980, when a Texas state agency decided to discontinue using EDS and hire a smaller New York agency that was cheaper and more technically diverse, Perot went to war with a vengeance. In what would later be recognized as vintage Perot, he compiled a thick dossier about his rival, as well as negative personal information about certain Texas officials who had been involved in the decision. He also said he believed there was a conspiracy among Texas officials to destroy the New York company and steal the business for themselves. When officials from the New York company began to receive anonymous threatening phone calls, they suspected it was part of Perot's campaign, but it couldn't be proved. In the end, Perot called in every chip he could muster at the state capital, with the governor and high-level officials—and he won. There are those who might congratulate his tenacity, but few people, in their hearts, can defend this way of doing business. Never forget that the people you deal with are not simply cardboard caricatures of their companies. They're real flesh and blood. They can suffer, be destroyed, and, in time, seek revenge.

❀ DON'T ABUSE YOUR POSITION

Think back to when you first started working. Do you remember the first person you encountered who made sure from the outset that you understood your "place" in the scheme of things? The person who watched you and made sure you did everything the "right" way (meaning his—or her—way)? The first person (besides your parents) to ever say, "Because I'm the boss, that's why"? This person may have been the eighteen-year-old night manager at a 7-Eleven or a petty dictator who managed the station where you pumped gas. But in your eyes that person was capable of making or breaking you.

The fact is, when you're in charge, you can pretty much make people jump as high as you want. But management by abuse, intimidation, or humiliation isn't really management at all. It's tyranny. It hurts people, makes their work life hell. The only way to gain respect—which is really what you're after—is to be respectful.

❀ *DON'T TAKE CRITICISM PERSONALLY*

As has been said, referring to Freud, "Sometimes a cigar is just a cigar." But sometimes when people criticize your product or your work, there is an awful wrenching in your gut and a feeling that the criticism is much, much more. It's a rejection that pierces the center of your being, a challenge to who you are as a person.

The truth is, every person in a position of authority will be criticized. If you let each insult draw blood, you'll be cut down in no time. And if you take every criticism of what you do as a direct personal challenge, by the time something really challenging gets in your face, you won't be able to distinguish it from any of the other challenges you're already dealing with. In other words: Hold your fire. Try to listen to the content of the criticism. Consider how you might react if it wasn't about you. Be curious instead of defensive, and you'll learn something.

Nine years spent on the siege of Troy. Two years before the Greeks could even evoke a favorable wind to set sail for the city. Things certainly moved at a different pace than they do today, as though everyone had all the time in the world. Did any of the Greeks ever look back over the sea and wonder how their wives and children, their parents and friends, were faring?

Between them, Agamemnon and Achilles bore responsibility for the lives of thousands of people. Yet all these responsibilities seem to have evaporated in the heat of their personal battle.

When the principal partners in a great enterprise are consumed with destroying one another in a fit of pique, what hope can there be for the success of that endeavor? Titanic egos tend conversely to reduce the size of the field they are fighting on. No matter how broad and universal the issue may initially have been, its importance is reduced by the whining babble that then surrounds it.

Even if the culture had not demanded it, the clash between Agamemnon, the king of men, and Achilles, the warrior King, would have been inevitable: no respect shown, no respect given, just insults and threats. The showdown between Agamemnon and Achilles could have happened yesterday in New York, Paris, or Hong Kong. Wherever people are vying for power, influence, or prestige, there is hostility. Conversely, wherever people are trying to get a job done the best way they know how, there is an inevitable spirit of cooperation.

4

BETRAYAL

*Blind with fury and wounded by the insult to
his honor, Achilles strikes back, using his influence
with the gods to betray his colleagues*

Aᴄᴛᴇʀ ɢɪᴠɪɴɢ his lovely consort, Briseis, over to Agamemnon's heralds, Achilles, distraught, leaves his tent. He
walks for miles along the shore, past the dark hulks of the
beached Greek ships of war and the surrounding encampments, finding his way only by the stars in the sky and the
phosphorent gleam in the water.

Not only does he care deeply for Briseis, he fears for her
treatment at the hands of Agamemnon. Agamemnon is
going to sully Briseis; he intends to possess her. Achilles
staggers far out among the crashing waves and slippery
rocks of the seashore, weeping and sending his cries across
the water. "Mother! You bore me doomed to live but for a
little season. Surely Zeus, who thunders from Olympus,
might have made that little glorious. It is not so. Agamem-

non, son of Atreus, has done me dishonor and has robbed me of my prize by force."

Thetis hears her son's cries in the depths of the sea and appears out of the mist and forms before him. "My son," she inquires softly, "why are you weeping? What is it that grieves you? Keep it not from me, but tell me, that we may know it together."

Being a goddess, Thetis already knows the whole story, but she listens silently as Achilles bitterly recounts the indignities that have been done him. Having worked himself into a state of high dudgeon, he rashly asks his mother to fly to Zeus's side and intercede with him to bring devastation upon Agamemnon's forces. In his fury, Achilles doesn't consider or no longer cares that Agamemnon's forces also happen to be his own friends and allies. His loss of face is his only concern.

"Bid Zeus to support the Trojans," he pleads. "Let the Greeks be hemmed in at the sterns of their ships and perish on the seashore."

Thetis, as hot-tempered as the child she bore, thinks only of her glorious son being insulted at the hands of Agamemnon and agrees to intercede with Zeus. Later, atop Olympus, she throws herself at Zeus's feet and spills out her heart's desire. And Zeus, though troubled by her request, loves Thetis dearly and cannot refuse her. He agrees to act against Agamemnon's army.

Now Achilles' act of betrayal is complete. On a higher, more noble level, Achilles knows that treason is the highest act of dishonor. But he has lost his focus on the mission to regain Helen. With no thought for the welfare of his comrades, without consideration for the morality of his request, Achilles thinks solely of the salve to his wounded pride. He believes that only in murder, mayhem, and defeat will the Greeks see how much they have lost by allowing this insult to Achilles to stand. They will realize that only Achilles can lead them to victory. They will be forced to come to him on bended knee and beg him to save them from utter destruction. They will offer him prizes beyond imagination. They will strip the failed leader Agamemnon bare and drag him alive around the walls of Troy to honor the savior of them all, Achilles.

Achilles' desire for retribution is directed solely at Agamemnon. The fact that its impact will resound throughout the ranks of Achilles' allies is of little consequence. Achilles' honor has been challenged; he is intent on respect, pride, his sense of place and import.

If one believes, as Achilles did, that man's place is fated and his destiny is preordained, Achilles' actions are only his actions, and whatever happens to individuals is out of his control. All lives are determined by the gods. His quarrel is with Agamemnon. If others die as a result of that quarrel, their deaths are meant to be. They are not his responsibility, nor are they of his making.

Even though Achilles is consumed with thoughts of revenge against Agamemnon, he is able to give a noble gloss to an ignoble action.

A Modern Parable:
Business as Usual, a Fraudulent Life

Not all betrayals occur in the heat of emotion. Sometimes it's just business as usual.

A brilliant bond trader on Wall Street began to capture the imagination of investor after investor after the trade portfolio he had built poured golden profits into his company's coffers quarter after quarter. This brilliant young investor amassed a huge base of financial support, as people began to believe that, with their money in his hands, they would realize nothing but enormous profit. And indeed, for a while everyone's dreams were realized.

In the process, something happened to the trader. In the course of a few years, he went from being just a savvy guy who saw a way to make a few bucks to being treated as an almost godlike guru of investment strategy. People begged him to take their money and do whatever he wanted with it. So he did. Everyone said he was a genius, a magic charm, and he started to believe it. He felt godlike.

He began to set up deals that required unimaginable sums to execute, deals that would assure him of obscene profits while tumbling to dust beneath him like a fragile house of cards, leaving the small investors with nothing. By the time anyone realized what had occurred, his profits were secure, the deals had crashed and burned, and he was able to walk away clean, saying, "Well, I tried my best. Investment is a risky business. Ah, well."

Still, people remained confident in the trader, kept giving him their money to invest. Again, the trader walked away richer and richer, while his investors were again left with almost nothing. Finally, the Securities and Exchange Commission began to examine his operations. He was found liable for double dealing and fraud, was fined hundreds of millions of dollars, and was jailed for a number of years.

Today, he is a free man, and still enormously wealthy. For a short time he was a bit of a social and business pariah, but rehabilitation is swift among the wealthy and powerful. The very people he had once defrauded and betrayed returned to him in force, and very soon he began to feel like a god again.

Lesson Four

The Shield of Integrity

We have become jaded in the presence of betrayal all around us: A top CIA agent sells secrets to the Russians; a fired automobile company executive turns over the plans for his former company's new car to a competitor; high-level political aides leave office and write damaging tell-all books about their former bosses; huge corporations try to ruin their critics by leaking sexual innuendos.

Is it betrayal when a company employing thousands of

workers unilaterally decides to cut expenses (jobs, plants) by outsourcing to nonunion suppliers or overseas manufacturers? Is it betrayal when the country's oldest and largest socially responsible mutual fund is sold behind shareholders' backs to people with questionable commitment? Is it betrayal when the producer of a metal used in technology knowingly exposes its workers to poisonous substances? Is it betrayal when an automobile manufacturer sends a minivan to market that has a potentially fatal flaw?

Talent without integrity is tragic. The force that grows inside the minds of tremendous egos who are ungoverned by any moral boundaries can wreak unimaginable havoc. Betrayal, whether it springs from arrogance, greed, or fury, seems justified in the perverse mind of the traitor.

In many respects, betrayal is the inevitable consequence of business environments that push for higher and higher levels of achievement without counting the costs, that extol the virtues of those who earn the most without looking at the true impact on others. Betrayal is arrogance—the knowledge that "I can ruin you if I choose to"—and the willingness to follow through. Usually, those who betray others don't blame themselves; they blame the object of their betrayal for being too weak to stop them.

Inside companies, betrayal is a silent cancer that feeds on ambition and fear. Personal betrayal is most likely to occur when things aren't going well and everyone is looking around for a fall guy. That's what happened to former Sony

Pictures Entertainment studio chairman Mark Canton when his boss, Alan J. Levine, publicly blamed him for Sony's huge losses. Canton was fired, but not before he had similarly tried to pass the buck to TriStar president Marc Platt.

These are big names in high-profile companies, and their dramas may seem to have little to do with normal business life. But on a smaller scale, betrayal exists whenever you blame a subordinate for a mistake you both failed to notice, or fire a productive worker merely to reap praise for creating a leaner department, or expose a secret a colleague has confided to you, or lie at someone else's expense in order to protect yourself. The new age at work requires integrity based on the simple principle that an effective workplace is one in which fairness and dignity are valued. The shield of integrity, your fourth piece of armor, is crafted from the following:

❀ PLAY FAIR

Fairness requires a fundamental respect for others, a sense of justice, and the ability to view situations comprehensively, not just through the narrow tunnel of your own wants and needs. You must decline to engage in activities that involve underhanded dealings or trickery.

Sometimes no one but you will know what is fair; it is at that moment that you may feel tested and tried, but cloaking yourself in a mantle of decency allows you to prevail over your or anyone else's baser instincts. That mantle of decency will shield you in times of anger and frustration, times when you feel wronged, times when your emotions are on the verge of overwhelming you.

❀ DON'T USE YOUR INFLUENCE TO BETRAY OTHERS

"It's good to be the king." But even if you are the king, maybe *especially* if you are the king, you set the tone by your behavior. It's easy to ruin reputations—an arched eyebrow, a look, a word—and not so easy to repair them. Be careful of whom you speak badly; sometimes viperish behavior nets you viperish behavior, and who wants to live or work in a nest of vipers?

❀ GUARD AGAINST BULLYING

A bully is someone who has the power to make life at work a torturous misery. If you have ever worked for a bully or with a bully, it is a singularly horrible, demeaning, resentment-building, ego-breaking experience. Bullies get their way by stepping on your independence, changing the rules midstream, or firing you if you don't toe their line. Bullying is an insidious form of betrayal. It is a breakdown of the human contract that is understood between employers and employees.

Sharon, a freelance graphic designer for a large advertising agency, had been working with the same art director for ten years. They had developed a good working relationship and even a friendship. Sharon was a talented designer, and she knew she was unusually prompt and cooperative—qualities that are valued greatly in the often crazed advertising world. One day, the art director called her in a panic. She had a rush job that had to be completed in two days. Could Sharon do it? Sharon balked. She honestly wasn't sure that two days was enough time to do a quality job. The art director was annoyed. "We're friends. I thought I could count on you," she said, missing the point. Again, Sharon tried to explain that she needed more time to produce the kind of work that met her standards—and, she thought, the agency's. Now the art director's voice turned cold. "I guess I'll have to get someone else," she said, and hung up the phone.

Sharon felt intimidated and depressed by the conversation. What kind of friend would be so bullying? After all, Sharon wasn't refusing the job; she was just being honest. But she could tell that the art director had taken her response as a personal slight. Sharon dreaded what was to come.

Two weeks later, when a project she was expecting didn't arrive, she called the art director to find out where it was. "Oh," her old friend said casually, "we decided to give that job to another designer." Sharon's heart sank. "Why?" she asked. "I don't understand." Now the art director's tone was all business. "Time constraints. I explained to everyone that you were too busy with other work to meet our dead-lines, so we've hired another freelancer to pick up the slack."

Sharon began to argue, but clearly it was of no use. The art director had the ultimate power, and she had decided to punish Sharon. Even after her ten years of diligent and creative work, Sharon was out—just like that. It was a petty grievance but a devastating betrayal.

❖ NEVER MAKE DECISIONS IN THE HEAT OF EMOTION

When it was learned that someone had leaked highly confidential details about Federal Reserve meetings before the feds released their economic report in September 1996, a shock ran through the financial community. The ripple was felt as far as Wall Street, which reacted to the news with a dip in the Dow Jones. The Federal Reserve decision-making process about whether or not to raise interest rates is a closed process. The implication of leaks was serious. Leaks of misinformation or disagreements among Federal Reserve banks could send the market into a flurry of un-warranted activity. Who could have broken this impor-tant code of silence? No one knows for sure, but there are suspicions that a disgruntled high-level official at a regional bank who disagreed with the feds' decision not to raise rates leaked his frustrations to a reporter. The individual involved could not have appreciated or cared about the damage inherent in his breach of faith.

Examples of betrayal, great and small, occur every day. The reaction "I'll get you for that!" resounds in the halls of many companies, whether spoken or unspoken. This reaction is the force of emotion conquering the force of reason. One of the most effective ways to process disappointment and rage is to reframe the incident in which you were offended. Practice stating clearly and forcefully how you feel, but leave the tone of rancor and accusation behind. You're more likely to get the response you want when you're honest without being abusive.

Achilles' act of betrayal was performed in the heat of uncontrollable rage. It was a bold *I'll show you* whose purpose was to appease his own sense of righteousness. But although he felt justified by Agamemnon's insults, it never occurred to him that by betraying Agamemnon he was also betraying his colleagues—and, perhaps most profoundly, himself.

5

WITHDRAWAL

*Having vowed to take his men and abandon
the war against Troy, Achilles sulks in his tent,
even as the Greeks face slaughter by the Trojans*

AGAMEMNON returns the maiden Chryseis to her father
and offers sacrifices to appease the anger of the god Apollo.
Apollo lifts the plague from the Greeks, and, now recovered, they once more prepare for battle.

The gods interfere again, and Agamemnon is sent a Lying
Dream of Victory, promising final success against the Trojans. But Agamemnon is unaware of Achilles' treachery.
Through Zeus, Achilles has laid the groundwork for the
humiliation and defeat of Agamemnon's forces before the
gates of Troy.

Achilles, meanwhile, remains cloistered in his tent, as he
"gnaws at his own heart, pining for battle and the war cry."
As promised by Zeus, the Greeks suffer blow after blow at

the hands of the Trojans. Knowing that Achilles and his men are nowhere to be seen on the battlefield, the Trojans swarm from behind their walls and press their advantage. Although Achilles is aware that his great skill as a warrior and a leader might turn the tide against the Trojans, he remains unmoved.

Achilles' men, the fierce Myrmidons, are forced to the sidelines as passive observers. The blow to their honor and pride is intense, but they are sworn to follow their leader. Were it only Achilles himself who stays from the battle, his decision might seem less grave. But he commands his troops to remain idle while old friends and colleagues die. It is demoralizing and shaming for the Myrmidons as they sit in helpless misery, listening to the battle rage from afar, seeing trails of smoke rise from the burning ships. In desolation they watch, knowing that if they ever return home and their children ask "What did you do in the great war against Troy, my father?" they can only reply, "We sat idle and watched the ships of our friends and allies burn."

In this way, the withdrawal and sulking of their leader brings shame and dishonor to all who follow him.

A Modern Parable:
Peevishness, Sulking, and Carrying On

Jack was a strong-willed and opinionated multimillionaire and a brilliant businessman, who procured a seat on the board of directors of a very powerful Fortune 500 Company by purchasing over 12 percent of its publicly offered stock.

Jack had always wanted to be on a large company's board of directors where he could make a significant contribution. This company was perfect. It was bristling with its own importance instead of getting down to the serious business of running the place right. Jack looked forward to putting his two cents in as to how things should be done to maximize profits and reinvigorate productivity—just like he'd done at the phenomenally successful company he'd built up from nothing, using his personal genius and innovative management techniques. And, indeed, the board of directors was delighted to have a man of such brilliant reputation and prestige on its board.

Of course, there was a firmly entrenched protocol for board meetings. The chairman, who was also the company's CEO, ran the meetings from a prearranged agenda. Everyone around the table (and these were men and women of great substance, leaders of industry in their own right) deferred to the chairman and made relatively conservative recommendations within the framework of the company's current operating policies.

Jack wasn't interested in protocol. At the first meeting he attended, he interrupted the chairman's report to lecture him about how he was plain wrong about key strategies. The chairman was polite but firm. "Perhaps our enthusiastic new member would like to put his ideas in a memo that we can review at a later meeting," he said, smiling.

His words were like a slap in the face to Jack, who wasn't accustomed to being challenged. Not only was he insulted, he was indignant. Did the company want to grow or didn't it? He thought he was there because the company wanted results, not for this silly glad-handing.

As the relationship between Jack and the chairman deteriorated, Jack started going behind the chairman's back, interviewing people in the company, speaking his mind to the press, and publicly blaming current leadership for the company's problems. Peevishly, he would tell reporters, "Why am I here if they aren't interested in building a better mousetrap? Don't they understand who I *am*?"

When his public outcries made no impact on the chairman or the rest of the board, Jack decided to use his powerful block of company shares to interfere with every decision the company made. He'd show them who had the power! Finally, because of a labor dispute that began as a result of his meddling in company policies, the stock began to plummet, and the company was forced to sell off two of its most profitable divisions to balance losses elsewhere in the company. Careers were destroyed, jobs were lost, economic hardship and decline were caused. Jack accepted no responsibility for any of this. Instead, he said, in effect, "I told you so," sold back his shares, and walked away. For years to come, his voice could be heard from the sidelines, complaining about how everything was the fault of those ineffective board members who just wouldn't listen to his good advice.

▣▣▣▣▣▣▣▣▣▣▣▣▣▣▣▣▣▣▣▣▣▣▣▣▣

Lesson Five

The Shield of Rigor

It's surprising how often we see and hear about leaders in business, government, sports, entertainment, and other fields behaving like sulky children who are peeved at not getting their own way. It is ironic that when an individual's sense of importance becomes inflated, the result is most often a tendency to revert to childlike behavior! Playing the demigod must be difficult, especially if the demigod doesn't receive the worshipful response expected.

Our culture is somewhat to blame for elevating people to such lofty positions. We worship sports stars even when they're crude, cantankerous, and uncooperative. We almost expect movie stars to be demanding and temperamental, stalking off film sets and brooding in their trailers if their fragile egos are bruised by any threat to their power or talent.

We also expect our tycoons to be quixotic, demanding, and insufferable. By our standards, people with a billion dollars can sulk all they want to! They can literally afford to sulk, if that is their wish. They can sulk loudly by calling press conferences and making pronouncements that the media is more than eager to report. Or they can sulk quietly, withdrawing and brooding. We don't condemn them. To quote Ovid, "As long as he is rich, even a barbarian is attractive."

Since we forgive our heroes their petty behavior, it becomes insinuated in our own businesses at every level. Petulance, sulking, withdrawal—these are the ultimate acts of irresponsibility for anyone in whom we place our trust. When a manager withdraws from the action and fails to be a leader, the rest of the staff is left to fend for themselves.

Clearly, if managers in today's companies were effective leaders, *The Dilbert Principle* by Scott Adams would never have reached first place on the best-seller list! Dilbert is the Everyman of the workplace, the embattled guy just trying to do his job in spite of his boss. In Dilbert's world, bosses are petty, peevish, malicious, obsessed with detail, and rarely there in a pinch. Dilbert has struck a public nerve—and it's not just the funny bone.

The new age at work requires concentration and dedication. You can't escape your problems; they don't go away. You must apply yourself to solving them. Your fifth shield is the armor of rigor. It is crafted from the following:

❈ STAY THE COURSE

An accountant recalls how his boss spilled coffee on someone's tax forms and got so peeved he just left the office and didn't come back for three hours. "I couldn't believe it. Then, when he finally came back, he told me to call the lady whose taxes he messed up and tell her there had been an accident—like *I'd* done it."

"My boss has a new brainstorm every day," an editorial assistant for a national magazine complained. "Just when I'm about to actually finish something, she'll come whipping in, drop a bombshell of an idea on my desk, then run off to a meeting. It's easy to have ideas, but she never thinks about what it might take to turn them into finished pieces."

These scenarios and others like them are so commonplace that there is even a web site devoted to boss horror stories.

Staying the course means taking personal responsibility. It means being there. It means not quitting when you run up against roadblocks. The most common grievances heard in offices today are about managers who can't abide any ripple in the smooth operation of their divisions—even though ripples are inherent in the job. In other words, they don't stay the course.

Rigor—the patience to remain steady through tough times, is exemplified by the Carolina Panthers, an expansion team in the National Football League. The management of the new Panthers organization believed strongly in a defined philosophy. Somewhat unique, it stressed qualities like accountability, not pointing fingers of blame at teammates, good character on and off the field, and unity in thought and leadership. The Panthers also wanted to win games, but the belief was that they *would* win if the players had character and leadership. In preparation for their first year, the Panthers spent an inordinate amount of time cultivating these qualities in the players. Critics of the Panther management who said they'd spent *too much* time seemed justified when the team lost its first five games. They might have fine character and great leadership, but what good did it do if they couldn't play the game?

There was intense pressure on the coach and the general manager to scrap the original strategy and just concentrate on football. Everyone wanted a win—they didn't care how. But even with their careers on the line, the coach and general manager decided to stick with what they knew was right. They went on to win seven of the final eleven games of their first season—an impressive record for a new team and even good for an old one.

❦ RISE ABOVE MOODINESS

Organizational life has its ups and downs. You wouldn't be human if you didn't get peeved or frustrated at times. And occasionally locking horns with your superior or having an idea shot down from on high are part of the landscape of corporate life. But being miffed doesn't give you permission to shut yourself in your office, refuse to take calls, and leave your staff wandering around outside waiting for direction. You might think you're punishing your boss by shirking your responsibilities, but you're also placing unfair burdens on the people who report to you. Nothing paralyzes an office faster than a moody manager, upbeat one minute and snarling the next.

The way you endure disappointment is just as important to leadership as the way you handle success. Most losses open up new opportunities, if you have the patience and discipline to stay the course.

❈ MORALE BUILDING IS JOB ONE

Managers aren't always aware of how much it means to people to be offered inspiration, hope, and encouragement—yet that's exactly what leadership is all about. Knowing what people need and giving it to them is like placing a glowing beacon at the end of a dark tunnel.

Inspiration isn't a vague concept, it's real. Consider the story told by U.S. Army General Bruce C. Clarke, shortly before his death, about an experience he had in World War II.

"During the Battle of the Bulge," Clarke recalled, "I visited a company of infantry that had lost all of its officers and a hundred men, and what was left of it was commanded by a sergeant—the first sergeant. And I tried to think of something to be encouraging. And finally I said to him, 'I got word that General Patton is turning north and is attacking in our direction.' And he looked at me and he said, 'If Georgie's coming, we've got it made!'"

Although General Clarke didn't know if General Patton or anyone else was actually coming to reinforce the shattered company, he inspired the first sergeant to continue fighting because Georgie was on the way.

General Clarke was awarded the Distinguished Service

Medal for his personal courage and outstanding leadership during the Battle of the Bulge.

Achilles chose to dwell on his grievances and sulk rather than exhibit a warrior's rigor. He brought shame to his men by holding them back from fighting in one of the greatest battles of their lives. His passivity in the face of urgent circumstances gave the lie to his mighty reputation. "Sulking Achilles" forever became a phrase associated with childish petulance and temper tantrums, a bad reaction to not getting one's way.

Managers and workers alike, we all come to a moment in our working lives when we must decide whether to commit fully to a choice or back away and ignore the opportunity to make a positive contribution. The moment we decide not to give our all, not to do what's fair, not to do what's right, we have lost the ability to fashion armor for the new age at work.

6

INFLEXIBILITY

*Agamemnon sends Ajax and Ulysses to
intercede and beg Achilles for an end to the quarrel
between them; Achilles remains unmoved*

AGAMEMNON begins to fear that victory against Troy is impossible. As his valiant soldiers fall before the Trojan warriors, as his armies suffer defeat after crushing defeat and are forced back to the shoreline, Agamemnon becomes certain that the gods have turned against him.

At the same time, the council of chieftains decides that it is Achilles' absence from the battlefield—along with Zeus's preference for Achilles—that is causing them to lose every encounter with the Trojans. They delegate Nestor to speak to Agamemnon on their behalf.

The sage Nestor, oldest of the Greeks and known for his wisdom, is direct with Agamemnon. He tells him that until he returns Briseis to Achilles, and sends messages of regret and conciliation as well as many splendid gifts, the losses among the Greeks will continue to mount. Appease Achilles at any cost, Nestor says, or all will be lost.

Agamemnon recognizes more than the truth in Nestor's words. The council of chieftains has sent a subtle but obvious message: If Agamemnon does not do as they say, they will take matters into their own hands. This is a crucial moment for Agamemnon. Does he rise, enraged, and tell them all that he will not be moved, that he alone is commander in chief? Or does he accept Nestor's implied threat and, before the entire council, accede to their wishes?

He bows his head and humbly admits, "I was wrong. I own it. I was blinded with passion and yielded to my worser mind." He then promises to send spectacular gifts to Achilles—gold and land and prize-winning horses and beautiful women, and the greatest spoils of all future battles. Finally, Agamemnon vows to return Briseis, saying, "I swear a great oath that I never went up into her couch, nor have I been with her after the manner of men and women."

Envoys are sent to Achilles—his friends Ajax and Ulysses. When they reach Achilles' tent, they find him sitting beside his devoted lifelong friend, Patroclus, playing on his lyre, singing haunting tunes of heroes past. Ulysses tells Achilles of Agamemnon's humble plea, his words of genuine regret and conciliation, as well as his promise of many gifts of great value and the return of Briseis. Ulysses recalls the loss of many of their comrades. Even if Achilles can't find it in his heart to forgive Agamemnon, he must pity the soldiers who are suffering so greatly. Ulysses is sure Achilles will rejoin the fight. He *must*. They need him!

But something has happened; something is wrong. Is this the Achilles that Ulysses knows? Achilles stares into Ulysses' eyes, his face a mask of stone. He is unmoved by the suffering of his friends and allies, unimpressed by Agamemnon's admissions of wrongdoing.

Ulysses' and Ajax's visit only underlines the righteousness of his position. Their coming to him now only makes him more angry. Why didn't the council of chieftains take his side in the first place? Did so many men have to die before they finally saw his worth?

Achilles scowls at his friends, feeling newly insulted by Agamemnon's pathetic ruse. It is not so easy to mend this great rift. His grudge uppermost in his mind, he says, "Let Agamemnon tempt me no further, for he shall not move me."

Agamemnon's insult has festered and grown. Now it is too deep a wound for Achilles to forgive. At the moment when he is offered more status, glory, and reward than ever, when Agamemnon himself begs forgiveness, he cannot overcome himself. It is the moment for Achilles to rise above petty emotion. But the moment is lost.

Achilles is rigid as stone, unyielding in his determination, sure that he is justified. Achilles is absolute and implacable. Achilles says no.

A Modern Parable:
Like a Rock, Stubborn to the Death

Tasty Frozen Foods was proud of its know-how and leadership. Decades earlier, Tasty had virtually invented the idea of frozen dinners, reading the post–World War II market with extraordinary vision. Somehow the innovative company leaders figured out that American homemakers wanted convenience along with quality. No longer were they willing to spend hours a day slaving over a hot stove. Furthermore, the family style was more casual; formal meals were out. Tasty coined the term TV Dinner for its initial line of individually packaged meals—containing meat, potatoes, sauce or gravy, vegetable medleys, and cake or pudding—reflective of the typical American evening meal for that time.

Tasty's market share was consistently commanding, even as other food manufacturers began to develop their own frozen-food product lines. Over the years, the dinners were modified in various ways, but they retained their signature big-tray design and generous portions.

Then one year, inexplicably, sales of TV dinners fell drastically. Was it a fluke, or had something changed? Tasty hired a market research company, which reported that consumers were increasingly interested in lighter foods with fewer calories and less fat. They found frozen dinners too fattening. There were a couple of ways to interpret the report: Either the new food trend was a passing fad, or they'd better get busy and come up with new options to meet the changing demand.

They decided it was a fad. With the vision of hindsight, it's easy to say it was a ridiculous posture to take. But you have to understand the mentality at work. Tasty Frozen Foods was not only king of the market, it *created* the market. If Tasty judged something to be a fad, it was a fad. You couldn't dominate a market for so long and miss a real trend.

Other frozen food companies, perhaps not as certain as Tasty, decided to hedge their bets. Soon low-calorie, low-fat, and small-portion frozen dinners were appearing on the shelves, right next to the standard products. Now consumers had a choice, and they started to make it. Tasty's research company discovered something that alarmed them: Not only were people buying the low-calorie, low-fat, small-portion dinners, they were also beginning to show a preference for product lines that included those choices—even when they purchased the regular versions. The bottom line was that Tasty's market share was falling like a rock.

Armed with this powerful information, the product development and marketing managers of Tasty took their recommendations to the executive committee. They told the executives that Tasty had to make changes—and fast. The executives listened silently, but when they were finished the chief financial officer, who had been with the company since its inception, stood up and gave his firm opinion that in order to continue being the market leader, the company had to stay firm and adhere to its signature products. "This health food craze will disappear," he said, "and all the companies that invested millions in making rabbit food will get hit hard." The president agreed, and so did the other executives.

The marketing director was adamant. "The market is changing. We have to change too." But the executive committee stood by its decision. Rigid, inflexible, sure, Tasty Frozen Foods marched forward into its certain future.

Lesson Six

The Shield of Flexibility

There are companies that become so powerful, so entrenched, that they are like dynasties, and their managements become like Mandarin emperors: remote, mysterious, aloof, godlike in their precious habits, their likes and dislikes. As one emperor dies, another rises to take his place and a new dynasty begins. It is never very different from the previous dynasty—just different faces, different costumes, different favorites.

These are the great and profound companies, the movers and shakers of both hardware and technology, the benders and shapers of cultural tastes and desires. They need not be named to be instantly brought to mind. They are so much a part of our lives that their brand names are the word for the object they produce. What they make is what we call it; what we call it is what they make.

Eventually, such companies develop a certain overconfidence. It's almost unavoidable. They operate a certain way, because that is what has always worked for them. This can be seen as an admirable trait. It's good to stick to your guns, to do things the way you do because it's the right way—until consumers make it clear that they want something else, which, sooner or later, they *always* do. A company that can't adapt to changing consumer demands is committing slow suicide, because someone else is going to meet that demand. Like an extinct species that once walked the earth, companies that can't adapt will eventually die.

In both the automotive and computer industries, there have been vivid examples of corporate refusal to accept clear signals, both of changes in the marketplace and in consumer demand. This has led to near disaster for two companies once considered invulnerable to any jolt of market forces. These companies managed to save themselves at the last minute, but it has been a painful process. Both are still re-tooling, changing the focus of their services in one case and of their products in another. Both are under new leadership and new philosophy, and "downsizing" is still a catchword in these formerly job-secure industries. Workers suffer for the sins of their leaders.

Inflexibility, the inability to respond to the forces of change, still makes many corporate cultures so rigid, so controlled, that they can't steer a new course no matter what, even if it's necessary for the very survival of their companies! They doom themselves by clutching at structures instead of at values, at the glories of the past instead of at new opportunities. Like the elderly who only long for life as it used to be, they stagnate in the memory of things that have ceased to be.

The new age at work requires an innovative mix of one part certainty and two parts flexibility. Movement is not optional; the only question is whether you're going to board the right train. Your sixth piece of armor, flexibility, will shield you from extinction. It is crafted from the following:

❀ NEVER SAY NEVER

There's no doubt that it's a good feeling to know where you're headed. Some people are obsessive about it: the planners, the chart makers, the list keepers. They're the ones who will show you a copy of a proposal you wrote last year to question why you're now saying something different. With the fervor of prosecuting attorneys, they'll use all your prior statements against you, giving you no room to maneuver.

Here's the problem with the flow-chart mentality: It bears little relationship to the way life really works. And that's more true than ever in these times of rapid change, technological explosions, and restructuring. You can only thrive if you *expect* things to change; you *expect* disruptions in the plan. Then you won't be thrown off course because you're walking a course with many dips and circles.

❀ FORCE INNOVATION

Japanese companies have a philosophy of *Kaizen*, which means "continuous improvement." In practice, *Kaizen* involves a carefully orchestrated system of change built into the foundation of operations. Every worker in a company is responsible for constantly finding better ways to produce a product, cut costs, or address market needs. In a *Kaizen*-driven company, it is impossible to stagnate. To quote a Zen saying, "There is always a larger game."

We can learn much from our global partners in different parts of the world. But we have to accept the challenge of innovation in order to do so. When American factory workers in joint ventures with the Japanese were first introduced to *Kaizen*, they dismissed it as a meaningless principle. But very shortly they were bursting with enthusiasm. There are two reasons. First, most workers want to achieve excellence. Second, when your company encourages you to be creative, come up with fresh ideas, and find ways to do things better—and they really listen to you—it's a great feeling.

❖ DON'T BE AFRAID TO ADMIT MISTAKES

Acknowledge your mistakes and move on. That's a tough thing for most managers to swallow, and you can understand why. When work environments are fiercely competitive, and jobs are on the line every day, nobody wants to admit to anything. (Some companies are so intimidating that people don't even want to be *noticed*.)

Our dysfunctional business culture has a funny attitude about mistakes. Although we all know that everyone makes them, we pretend that only incompetent people do. This is most evident in public life. We mock public officials when their programs don't work, even if we were all for them six months earlier. We are unforgiving of any black marks we find in a public official's life—mistakes that were made dozens of years ago and weren't even significant then. In corporate life, the fear of admitting mistakes is not as obvious, but it's deeply ingrained in the culture. However, when you can't admit mistakes, you can't progress. Life becomes an unraveling series of cover-ups and pretense.

Perhaps the attitude of the Saturn Corporation is a sign that companies are beginning to reevaluate the way they represent their products. Traditionally, companies have been rigid about their products, defending them to the death even when there are clear (and sometimes dangerous) problems. The public perception was that companies couldn't be trusted—one reason we have such powerful regulating agencies. Saturn has handled recalls without hysteria and without excuses, as a way of admitting that mistakes happen and the company is on the front lines, solving the problems on the spot. The first crisis came only a month after the first Saturns were sent to market. The company discovered a flaw in the front seat recliner mechanisms. With unprecedented speed, Saturn found the problem, voluntarily recalled 1,480 cars—contacting each customer by overnight mail—and briefed dealers by closed-circuit television. The recall went so well that Saturn made a further bold step. The company actually *used the recall in its advertising*. Why would they do that, remind people that they made a mistake? The reason Saturn did it—and the reason why it was such a successful marketing idea—was to show how Saturn would turn the world upside down to take care of its customers.

This flexible approach to business is in direct opposition to companies that advertise, "We never make mistakes. Our products never have problems." Consumers already know that no product is 100 percent infallible. What they're really interested in knowing is what you'll do for them if something goes wrong.

❋ CHOOSE YOUR ADVISERS CAREFULLY

Seek honest opinions from your superiors and your staff. The way people think and feel serves as an important piece of research in the decision-making process. Don't, however, take everything you are told at face value. Sometimes people shade the truth in order to flatter their bosses, or they'll tell you what they think you want to hear. Reflect on the advice others give you. Consider the source. Is the person reliable? Is the advice self-serving? Does it seem to be a rehash of something you've already tried? What are the potential benefits and risks?

In addition, choose a mentor or a confidant—someone in the company whom you trust completely. That person is probably not your supervisor and might even be someone in another division. The most successful executives have good advisers. They understand that tough decisions require more than one mind.

❧ DON'T SUBMIT TO FATE

In Greek mythology, fate's will and free will could not coexist. Organizations are not like that. There is no such thing as an inevitable result or an absolute knowledge of the future.

As a manager, it's important to realize that this is true of individuals, as well. A degree from a prestigious business school doesn't guarantee a great employee. Nor does a lack of standard credentials mean a person can't do an excellent job. If an employee makes a mistake once, that doesn't mean he or she is fated to make it over and over. In a world of fate, each person operates in a closed circle of predestined limits. In a world of flexible management, everyone has an opportunity to excel beyond all expectations—if you let it happen.

Achilles' pride made him implacable, rigid, hard as stone. Because he filtered all advice and information through a narrow screen of anger, he was unable to hear what his friends were offering. Nor could he feel any empathy for their plight. Because he was so certain of his position, he was not satisfied with words of concession. It was his choice to remain alone and absolute as others forged ahead. There is nothing sadder than a person who is so certain of the one way. Finally, Achilles was left alone as the others chose a different path.

7

DECEIT

*Patroclus, girded in Achilles' armor, convinces Achilles
to let him lead the Myrmidons into battle,
while Achilles remains in his tent*

THE TROJANS, emboldened when they realize Achilles has
withdrawn from the siege of Troy, decide to press their sudden advantage. Without Achilles, Agamemnon's armies
have been falling back before the probing strikes of the Trojans. Without the sight of Achilles in the vanguard, wreaking havoc on the enemy, the Greek forces quickly become
disheartened and suffer defeat after defeat. As Achilles sees
the dead and wounded dragged by his tent on litters, it
troubles him that he is unable to come to his allies' aid.

It never occurs to him that he *could* help them if he chose
to, but his pride and wounded honor won't allow it. Two
of his oldest friends are dragged by. He hears their moans
and comes to the edge of his tent to watch them. His eyes

fill with tears at the sight of his friends, so gravely wounded, groaning in pain and shock.

Achilles' closest friend, Patroclus, is also strongly swayed by the dire circumstances of his fellow Greeks. Patroclus begs Achilles to lead the Myrmidons into battle, but Achilles' honor will not permit it. Patroclus refuses to let it rest at that. They have spent nine endless years in this pursuit, and now, when the Trojans finally come out from behind their walls and fight, Achilles stays in his tent, brooding.

Patroclus knows how dire the situation has become; he has visited the other camps and seen the dead and dying, the despair everywhere. His hope is to inspire the dispirited Greeks to fight on. And then it comes to him: the perfect solution. He respects Achilles; he understands his position. But now is not the time to hesitate. Now is not the time to hold back, to withdraw.

Begging Achilles to listen to him, Patroclus lays out his daring plan. What can go wrong? Achilles can maintain his position, and his honor will remain unsullied. Patroclus offers greater glory to his friend's name and legend; he convinces the reluctant Achilles to let him, Patroclus, don the trademark armor. When the Trojans see the famous armor and chariot of Achilles flying at them, they will believe that Achilles has relented and returned to the battle, and they will flee in terror. The Greek forces will also be roused by the sight of the great Achilles and rejoin the fray with renewed fervor. This ruse by itself might be enough to save the day. Desperate measures are needed, he argues.

Achilles is reluctant, but Patroclus persists. Forcing Achilles to the front of the tent, he opens the flap and shows his friend that the Trojans are advancing to the Greek ships themselves and are setting them afire.

Alarmed by the Trojans fighting only feet from his tent, and moved by his dear friend's passionate conviction, Achilles agrees to lend Patroclus his famous armor. He cannot throw aside his vows and fight himself, but he outfits his dear Patroclus in the magical armor and allows him to lead the Myrmidons in an onslaught against the swarming Trojans.

Patroclus, transformed by Achilles' armor, performs extraordinarily, and he succeeds in repelling the Trojans almost entirely. In the terrifying, gleaming armor of Achilles, he drives them away from the Greek ships and back to the walls of Troy. So successful is Patroclus that he surges way beyond the Myrmidons and is soon completely surrounded by the enemy. They slay his horses and overturn his chariot, spilling him to the ground, but he fights on. He slaughters so many of the enemy that he is standing on a pile of dead bodies when he comes face to face with Hector, prince of Troy and greatest of all Trojan warriors.

The Trojans, thinking they have trapped the mighty Achilles, form a fighting pit around the Greek and their prince. Patroclus is weary; he has been fighting for hours. His arms feel so heavy he has trouble drawing Achilles' sword from its scabbard. Hector looks huge to him; the Trojan hardly seems tired at all. There is no way out. Wherever Patroclus looks, he sees mobs of Trojans, jeering and yelling insults.

The god Apollo, favoring Troy, flies down from Olympus to watch the contest. He has waited a long time to see Achilles bested by Hector. When he sees that it is only Achilles' friend Patroclus, masquerading as the greatest of the Greek warriors, Apollo is astonished and decides to have some fun to assuage his disappointment. As Patroclus raises his arm to strike at Hector, Apollo knocks Achilles' helmet from Patroclus's head and Achilles' golden lance from his hand. Now it is clear to the Trojans that this is not Achilles. A mighty jeer rises from the Trojans' throats.

Patroclus, his disguise gone, revealed as Achilles' surrogate, tries to run but is pushed back to the center of the circle. He reaches down to retrieve the lance Apollo has knocked from his hand, only to have a Trojan foot soldier fling a spear into his lower back. Arching up in pain and surprise, Patroclus grasps the deadly spear and pulls it from his back. Thus distracted, he is unable to defend himself from Hector, who at this moment steps forward and, with one sudden movement, eviscerates Patroclus with another spear.

Startled, Patroclus drops to his knees, his hands clutched to his lower belly as his intestines spill from him. He looks up—just long enough to see Hector's sword poised above him. The rest is a flash of light into total darkness.

Patroclus dies—victim of the god Apollo's continued treachery, victim of Hector's spear, victim of his best friend Achilles' pride.

A Modern Parable:
A Personal Deception

Gerald's state-of-the-art electronics company had been going great guns for almost three years, and it was starting to attract attention. Of course, when you're just beginning, everyone works hard—and for Gerald's employees that meant weekends and evenings. The pay wasn't quite up to speed, but he was certain it would be, once he settled some of the company's debts.

Gerald felt he owed a lot of credit to Mark, his partner and operations manager. The two men had known each other for over twenty years, had worked together and become social friends. When Gerald had asked Mark if he'd like to come on as a full partner, Mark had jumped at the chance. It was the opportunity of a lifetime for the talented electronics whiz. And Mark was quite impressed with the numbers Gerald ran by him. The deal looked financially sound, not a high-risk venture like most new companies.

In the last few months, Mark had noticed that his friend was looking unusually drawn and tired. He asked Gerald several times if he was feeling okay, and Gerald always assured him that he was. "I'm just a little tired, that's all." Mark didn't press him, but he had a feeling it was something more than that. From time to time, he'd walk into Gerald's office to find him engaged in heated conversations on the phone, his face colored to a red hue that seemed part fear and part pain. Mark was on the verge of seriously confronting his friend when he received a midnight call from Gerald's adult son. The news was unthinkable: Gerald had committed suicide earlier that evening. Choking back tears, his son told Mark how they had found him lying on the bathroom floor, a bullet hole through his head. A note was found on the dresser in the bedroom, saying only, *I'm sorry . . . I love you.*

Mark was consumed with feelings of guilt. He'd known something was wrong, he should have acted. His poor friend. How he must have suffered!

The next morning, Mark managed to pull himself together and go to the office, where he knew he would be needed. After gathering the employees for a sober announcement, he went into Gerald's office and closed the door. He still could not fathom the reason for Gerald's despair.

He was soon to learn. Within days of Gerald's death, federal agents showed up at the office and abruptly confiscated all the financial files. The next week was a nightmarish unveiling of one shock after another. Gerald had failed to pay withholding taxes of over $100,000. He had borrowed to the hilt and defaulted on a major loan. The apparently healthy little company was in debt to the tune of over $3 million; the trail of deception and fraud seemed endless. And everyone was looking at Mark.

It had never occurred to Mark to get involved in the finances of the company. That was Gerald's area, and Mark had no reason to doubt that everything was in excellent shape. But now he learned that *he* was responsible for everything. He was a partner. His name was on every piece of paper. Suddenly, not only was Mark ruined financially, but the feds were anxious to pin the tax rap on him. Barely able to comprehend the scope of his troubles, Mark sometimes thought that Gerald had taken the easy way out.

Lesson Seven

The Shield of Honesty

Deceit is the last resort of the coward. It is often an act of desperation—weaving a tangled web while convincing oneself that everything will work out in the end. Deceit doesn't discriminate between friend and foe. Everyone gets caught in the web.

There are countless examples in history, literature, and film of people whose desperation led them to deceive the people closest to them.

Your seventh shield is the armor of honesty, crafted from the following:

❊ *DON'T LET OTHERS TAKE THE FALL FOR YOU*

A cowardly manager will do everything possible to escape having to perform unpleasant or difficult tasks. Wade's boss was such a person. Wade was a competent and loyal manager working for a large HMO. One day his boss called him into her office and told him she was promoting him to an executive position. He'd deserved it. He was loyal, hardworking, and well liked in the company. She wanted Wade to be a more important part of the HMO's growth. Wade was delighted, and his friends in the company were very happy for him. But less than a month after his promotion, Wade learned there was going to be a major downsizing of middle management positions in the company that would affect many of his former peers. Once again, the boss called him in. She told Wade it was a very difficult thing to eliminate people's jobs, but it was one of those unavoidable responsibilities that fell in the laps of executives. She gave Wade the task of giving the bad news to his former colleagues, assuring him they'd take it better from a friend.

At first, Wade balked. Shouldn't the managers' own bosses give them the news? No, she told him, everyone concurred they wanted him to handle it. Reluctantly, Wade agreed. He called the managers into his office one at a time, told them their positions were being eliminated, and explained the severance package they would be receiving. In every case, not only were the managers stunned to learn they were being eliminated, they were also upset that they were hearing the news from Wade. Weeks ago, he'd been one of them. Now he was firing them. It didn't seem right. Why weren't their own bosses doing it?

Resentment and rumors buzzed through the company.

Before they left, the fired managers let everyone know they thought Wade was power mad and he'd only been promoted because he'd agreed to be the company's hatchet man.

Three months after the firings, the company conducted an employee attitude survey. The results of the survey revealed that Wade was held in low regard and was not trusted by the workers. Based on this perception, Wade's boss decided it was in the best interests of company morale to let him go. A pink slip was Wade's reward for shouldering the other executives' distasteful obligations.

❀ DELEGATE AUTHORITY RESPONSIBLY

Achilles knew that, even protected by his mighty armor, Patroclus was no match for the Trojans. Only Achilles himself stood a chance of defeating them. So why did he let his friend go? Because he was determined not to go himself? Because he was too weak to say no? Because his emotions ruled? Perversely, because he loved Patroclus? All of the above? Leaders who don't know how to delegate responsibly—that is, who deliberately put someone in charge who is not qualified—are weak leaders. Strong leaders know how to delegate in a way that protects everyone's interests.

Erwin, the sixty-seven-year-old founder and president of a successful publishing company in Georgia, was planning to retire when he reached age seventy. He wanted to keep the company in the family so he brought in his son, Jeffrey, a newly minted MBA from a prestigious business school. Erwin figured that, although Jeffrey didn't know the first thing about publishing, he knew about business and he'd learn fast. He made Jeffrey the executive vice president, second in charge beneath Dad. Within a year, Erwin had named Jeffrey president and had taken a backseat to the everyday company business. Everything seemed to be going fine—until some of his best editors, people who had been with him for many years, started resigning. When he tried to find out why they were quitting, Jeffrey answered, "They're great people, Dad, but they're old and stuck in their ways. They couldn't accept our new direction."

It took a long time for Erwin to unravel the mystery. The "new direction," which Jeffrey had declared autocratically, defied some of the most sacred tenets of publishing, most notably insisting that editors would now cooperate with advertising executives to give favorable coverage to clients. It made perfect sense to Jeffrey, whose ignorance of publishing was only exceeded by his refusal to listen to the advice of the old hands and by his air of superiority, which cast a gloomy pall on the formerly spirited company.

Who was to blame for the mess? Ultimately Erwin, although it would have been much easier to blame Jeffrey, because he was heartily disliked by everyone. But it was Erwin who had dropped the ball, by sending his son into battle without training.

❖ *BE HONEST*

Avoidance is a form of dishonesty. It's a way of communicating that you can't deal with the messy business of delivering bad news. Psychologists might call it a form of passive aggressive behavior, something like: "I'm not going to tell you anything is wrong—I'm going to pretend to care—but when things fall apart, I'll be nowhere to be found." Amanda was a victim of this form of slithery dishonesty.

After eight years of working out of her home for a firm based in another state, Amanda was fired late on a Friday afternoon. The way it was done was inexcusably cowardly.

Although Amanda had separate telephone lines for family and business, Amanda's only answering machine was connected to her office line, so her teenage children's friends used the machine to leave messages. That Friday, Amanda's son Travis came home from football practice at about 6 P.M. His mother was making a late visit to a client, and he went to Amanda's office to check for messages. There was only one.

> Amanda, this is Carl. I'm sorry to have missed you, but I thought it was important to let you know about a decision we've made. We've been looking at a number of ways to cut costs. This morning, we decided that with the addition of the new software, we can manage without your services. I'll be unavailable until next

Thursday, but give me a call so we can arrange for you to ship our records and equipment back, okay? I'm really sorry about this. Good luck, and keep in touch. *Beep!*

Imagine Amanda's shock and embarrassment to arrive home and be told by her son that she'd been fired . . . on the answering machine! But what really galled her was that she'd talked to Carl earlier that day. He'd never even hinted that this was coming. And he *knew* she'd be out that afternoon because she'd told him about the client. He deliberately chose to call at a time when he could deliver the bad news without having to deal with any human consequences.

Another manifestation of indirect dishonesty is the manager who is consumed with the need to be perceived as a "nice guy." This manager can't stand conflict of any kind. Restaurant chef Jackie had a boss like that. He always walked around with a smile on his face, and whenever she asked his opinion about a dish she was preparing , his answer was always the same: "Great, great!" That's why she was astounded when he told her, with a contrite air, "It isn't working out." He explained that he wanted the cuisine to have more of a southern flair, very different from the kinds of foods she was preparing. Jackie's protest, "But you never *told* me!" died on her lips. He was already out the door.

One of the greatest tragedies in life is when someone close to you is destroyed by your hand. The blood on your hands may be invisible to the outside world, but it's there nonetheless. Achilles would come to realize that he had sacrificed his friend to the gods of death, but by then it would be too late. Once set in motion, deception is like a boulder torn loose from its moorings. No force of nature can stop its rapid, terrible descent.

8

VENGEANCE

*Patroclus is slaughtered; the wrath
of Achilles is unleashed*

THE DEATH OF PATROCLUS brings the already fevered
battle to a new pitch. Both sides hotly contend for his body.
Hector strips Achilles' beautiful armor from the dead man
and puts it on in place of his own before rejoining the fray.
A wild cry of approval erupts from his fellow Trojans as
Hector strides again into battle, now clad in the famous
gleaming armor of the great Achilles. The Greek forces,
seeing not only the valiant Patroclus killed but now Achilles' god-struck armor dishonored, let out a heartrending
cry of their own. So savage is the combat that a red mist
of blood mixes with the sweat and muck; it causes a crim-
son rainbow to rise in the air. Patroclus's naked corpse is
dragged back and forth between battling clots of Greeks

and Trojans, supported and pressed on all sides by masses of opposing troops hacking at one another, the wounded and dying fallen everywhere. In the midst of this blood heat, Zeus tosses an enveloping black mist over them all to add terror and confusion to the horrible turmoil. In a frenzy of frustration, the giant Greek warrior Ajax bellows to the heavens for intercession, and it is granted long enough for a messenger to be sent to Achilles to inform him of the fate of Patroclus. When the mist is lifted, the Greeks see it as a favorable omen and fight with renewed fervor, finally recovering Patroclus's ravaged corpse.

Achilles is at first disbelieving and then grief-stricken when he hears the news. The realization that he has allowed his dearest friend to fight in his place, and thus caused his death, is too much for him. In shock, he begins to call out for Patroclus again and again. He collapses to the floor of his tent and howls to the heavens. What has he done? How could he have allowed this to happen? What was he thinking, to let Patroclus wear his armor and lead the Myrmidons into battle! Why hadn't Achilles' men kept him from harm? Couldn't they see that he was no Achilles, that he needed to be protected, guarded? Achilles is filled with loathing and self-reproach for his behavior. His anger grows to a raging madness.

Thetis hears her son's cries from the depths of the ocean and appears to try to comfort him. But she is too late. Achilles is inconsolable. Weakened by his grief, pale, shaken, sick to his very soul, Achilles vows personal revenge on Hector for the death of Patroclus.

After nine endless years, the Trojan War is now, finally, a matter of blood vengeance. Achilles grabs a sword and a lance and is about to rush from his tent to find Hector and kill him when Thetis throws herself at her son's feet and begs him to control himself. Fearing that Achilles will be killed if he returns to battle now, Thetis persuades him to wait until she has procured a new suit of armor from Vulcan*, the blacksmith and armorer of the gods, to protect him in battle. Though shaking with rage and grief, Achilles once more submits to divine decree and agrees to wait until morning to seek out Hector and destroy him.

At dawn the next day, Thetis brings a gleaming new suit of armor to Achilles. It is still hot from Vulcan's forge, and gives off bolts of lightning as it lies at Achilles' feet. Donning the god-crafted armor, Achilles calls the leaders of the Greeks to council.

When the council has assembled, Achilles tells them that whatever problems there may have been between him and Agamemnon are over. He takes full blame for everything that's gone wrong since their quarrel began. Hanging his head, Achilles grieves for all the deaths and misery he has caused.

Everyone is stunned. Achilles has never behaved like this before. He is humble, modest, apologetic; most of all he is sad, full of grief and regret at the loss of Patroclus. Tears in his eyes, his voice rising into a cry of rage, Achilles then urges them to join him in renewed battle with the Trojans.

*Also known in the Greek as Hephaestus

With a huge roar of assent, they rush to their encampments to prepare for combat.

Now when Achilles goes into battle, it is with one thought alone: revenge. As he mounts his chariot and courses forward, Achilles' own horse turns and warns him (speaking for a god, of course) of his impending doom, but Achilles is not dissuaded. Hacking a swath of destruction through the Trojan troops, Achilles is mad with rage, screaming "Bring me Hector!" as he surges forward. He fights so fiercely that he single-handedly forces the entire Trojan army to turn tail and run. King Priam mounts the walls of his fortressed city, only to see his troops fleeing toward him, driven like cattle by the wrath of Achilles.

Hector, Priam's son, prince of Troy, is the only Trojan who stands before the gates and awaits the approach of Achilles. His parents can see the vast carnage that Achilles has created in driving the Trojans before him. They beg Hector to withdraw, to enter the gates and be safe behind the walls, but he refuses. How, after all, can he seek refuge from a single foe?

While Hector has turned to argue with his parents, Achilles approaches, "terrible as Mars, his armor flashing lightning as he moved." Hector is wearing the armor of Achilles that he tore from Patroclus's body after killing him the day before. Distracted by the pleas of his parents, he almost forgets Achilles is coming until his chariot pulls up right behind him.

"Hector," Achilles calls out, "where did you get such

beautiful armor? It doesn't look like it fits you. Turn and let me see how my armor looks from the front. Come, Hector. Turn and die."

Hector's back is to Achilles. He stands frozen, startled for a moment, then spins around and looks into Achilles' face. At the sight of him, Hector completely loses his nerve and runs.

Achilles pursues Hector endlessly round the walls of Troy, until finally—the gods intervening and tricking him—Hector turns and faces Achilles, realizing that his moment of death is at hand. His thrown spear bounces off Achilles' impenetrable shield; he draws his sword and lunges, only to find Achilles' lance piercing his throat. As he lies dying, he begs Achilles to return his body to his family for proper burial.

Achilles refuses. Did they return Patroclus's body willingly, honorably? No! This is the killer of Patroclus. This is the Trojan who stripped Achilles' armor from his dead friend's body and then had the temerity, the gall, to wear it. No, Achilles is hardly done with Hector. Instead of returning the dead man to his family, he strips his body and ties him to the back of his chariot by the heels. Then he drags Hector around the walls of Troy, to make sure his family and friends get a good look at him. He then drags Hector around Patroclus's funeral bier, to comfort and appease his dead friend's soul.

At last, the Greeks busy themselves with funeral rites for the war dead. They burn Patroclus's body on a high bier.

Then, following custom, they engage in games of strength and skill, make burnt offerings, and feast. Finally, drunk and full of meat, all fall to rest.

All but one. Achilles does not rest. He does not join the games; he does not eat or drink at the feast. Achilles cannot stop grieving. Thoughts of Patroclus consume him. Before dawn's light, Achilles ties Hector's body once again behind his chariot, and he drags the tortured corpse twice round the tomb of Patroclus, finally leaving the body face down in the dust.

The gods have been observing this from on high, and they are not pleased. The god Apollo, ever favoring Troy, sees to it that Hector's body remains undefiled by the harsh treatment meted out by Achilles in his frenzied rage.

The great Zeus hears the lamentations from both the Greeks and Trojans and sees the agony of Achilles. In an act of pity, Zeus sends Thetis to Achilles with a message of soothing compassion, hoping to heal Achilles' pain at the loss of Patroclus. Zeus also decides that Hector's ancient father, King Priam, should come to Achilles as a supplicant, bearing rich ransom, and beg the return of Hector's body.

In this way, Zeus hopes to appease the wrath of Achilles as well as teach him a lesson about decency and compassion. King Priam is transported to Achilles' tent with the god Mercury* as his guide and protector, so no harm may

---

*Also known in the Greek as Hermes

befall him. The old man throws himself before the great warrior's feet, kisses the same hands that killed his son, and begs for mercy.

As all the gods watch from Olympus, Achilles' eyes fill with tears and he rises from his couch, gently lifting the old man up before him. Without another word, Achilles embraces the old king, and gives him mantles and a robe with which to wrap his son's body. He accepts without looking at them the rich gifts brought as ransom and arranges for Hector's corpse to be brought to Priam.

Possessed of this spirit of repose and compassion, Achilles pledges a truce of twelve days to permit proper funeral rites.

The wrath of Achilles has been stilled, but only with the intercession of Zeus and far too late. The innocents who have died are mere pawns in another's game, cut down to feed another's fate and satiate another's desire for revenge. Their lives are gone and can never be returned. There is no compensation for the loss.

A Modern Parable: Revenge, a Hot Fire

Evelyn was one of thirty telephone operators for a busy airline office. She handled over a hundred calls a day on the airline's 800 number. That may seem like a lot, but her office's policy was that operators were to try and finish each call in five minutes. It was a high-pressure environment, especially since the airline expected the phone operators to sell tickets. If a caller was just price shopping and wasn't ready to make a reservation, it was considered a wasted call. In five minutes' time, Evelyn and her coworkers were expected to check schedules, find the best price deals, and write the tickets. They were to be friendly and helpful but at the same time speedy.

Evelyn was a diligent worker, but it was in her nature to be nice to other people and to be fair. When she was dealing with a potential customer, she really tried to help that person get the best deal—even if it meant recommending another airline, which she did on the sly, at times when her supervisor wasn't lurking around.

Of course, it wasn't always so easy to know when she was being watched. The supervisors had the authority to randomly listen in on the operators' calls. Evelyn considered this eavesdropping an insult to her dignity, and it put her constantly on edge. Almost every time her supervisor monitored her calls—about twice a week—she called Evelyn in for a critical review. She admonished Evelyn for being too slow and for not writing enough tickets. However, the supervisor had not yet caught her suggesting another airline.

It was bound to happen. One day Evelyn was called in to find her supervisor sitting behind her desk in a towering rage. Barely controlling her anger, the supervisor informed Evelyn that she had heard her recommending a competing airline to a potential customer—a very severe offense.

Evelyn didn't agree. She tried to explain the circumstances, how the caller had needed a completely different schedule from the one they offered, and how Evelyn thought it made the airline look good to make alternate suggestions, even if it meant that the caller chose another airline. The supervisor didn't care about Evelyn's altruistic impulses. She fired Evelyn on the spot.

Evelyn was stunned. She'd worked for the airline for five years. She had two young children at home. Where was she going to get another job? The more she brooded about it, the more furious Evelyn became. Was this what America had come to—treating workers like cattle in a pen, encouraging them to be dishonest to customers, firing them for performing acts of kindness? Was the company slogan, Customers First, a lie? She decided to do something about it. She called a local television reporter, who produced a nightly investigation of shocking business practices, and told her the whole story—embellishing it somewhat to highlight the coldheartedness of the supervisors and the extreme tension workers felt, knowing their calls were being monitored. She also described how she was dismissed after five years of loyal service, without even receiving severance pay. The segment ran on the evening news two weeks after Evelyn was fired, and it generated a huge response. The airline's spokesman was forced to give a public explanation. Even the president of the airline was backed into a corner. He agreed to see that Evelyn got severance pay, and he said if such business practices were occurring in his company he'd put an end to it. Of course he didn't do that. But he *did* fire Evelyn's supervisor, which was sweet revenge for Evelyn.

Bill's supervisor wasn't so lucky. Bill was a new hire in the same bank of operators. He was an edgy guy—probably too edgy to be working in such a high-pressure job. It was physically and mentally painful to Bill the way his supervisor was always breathing down his neck. She harassed him—made him feel like a fool. His rage bubbled beneath the surface, growing more toxic with every insult. And then his boss fired him for no reason. She just didn't like him. Bill had experienced problems at other jobs, but this was the final straw. Two days after he was fired, he walked into the airline office, pulled out a gun, and shot his supervisor twice in the chest.

Lesson Eight

The Shield of Respect

There is a sense of unease in many companies today, and for good reason. Time and again we see workers snapping under pressure and seeking their vengeance for perceived mistreatment in extreme and highly explosive ways. Violence is the number-one killer in the workplace. According to a 1994 American management survey of 311 companies, over 50 percent of them reported that one or more of their employees had been threatened, attacked physically, or killed on the job during the preceding four years. In 1992, the Bureau of Labor Statistics reported that 1,004 workers were murdered on the job —a 33 percent increase over the annual average during the 1980s. Of those murdered, 177 were managers. Moreover, a Northwestern National Life Insurance Company study found that 25 percent of all full-time workers were personally subjected to workplace violence between July 1992 and July 1993. Besides the emotional toll and human suffering, it was estimated that violence cost American companies about $4.2 billion in 1992, and there is no evidence of any downslide today. These are shocking statistics, implying that our culture of violence has finally come home to roost in the very places where we once felt physically secure.

Make no mistake, crazed employees will often follow through on their threats. In October 1994, Robert Begley, who had been fired from James River Corporation eight years earlier, was allowed inside the company's headquarters. He rode the elevator to the executive floor, where he pulled out a 9mm pistol and shot Brenton F. Halsey Jr., a vice president and son of a company founder, eight times, killing him. Then Begley killed himself. This tragedy occurred despite Begley's reported history of threatening company executives—for which he had once spent thirty days in jail.

The most visible episodes of violence often involve highly intensive work environments. The recent rash of postal worker shootings is a good example. You have to wonder why postal workers are so often provoked into explosive action. Is it the Civil Service structure that's at fault? Are the drivers, sorters, and carriers under too much pressure from their supervisors, who are under too much pressure from their postmasters to move a certain amount of mail and freight every day? Is the culture of the post office too rigid and inattentive to the needs of its employees? When workers or former workers show up at post offices with shotguns and assault rifles, we have to question what's going on in these places. We can no longer shrug violence off as the work of a handful of "crazy" people. It's a serious problem.

There is another kind of vengeance that occurs even more frequently than violence. Disgruntled workers purposely sabotage their work or the work of others as a way of punishing the company for bad treatment, unfair practices, or unpleasant working conditions. Theft of materials and/or money is estimated to cost American companies as much as $2.2 billion annually. Many workers justify theft as an acceptable payback for a company's failure to compensate them properly. They don't even consider it unethical, much less illegal.

There are also many reported instances of industrial sabotage: workers improperly assembling or installing crucial structural components of products as a way of punishing management for perceived or actual mistreatment of the laborers. There are work slowdowns, where employees are deliberately unproductive. All forms of sabotage—direct or indirect—demonstrate that the basic contract of cooperation and decency has broken down between companies and the people they employ.

Your eighth shield is the armor of respect, crafted from the following:

❊ *TREAT YOUR WORKERS LIKE HUMAN BEINGS, NOT MACHINES*

Even the best workers grow demoralized in the face of poor conditions. We all know that working for some managers can be comparable to being in prison. You feel trapped and claustrophobic. You are treated indifferently at best and mockingly at worst. Your talents and potential go unappreciated. Every workday seems like doing time in a dark and dingy cell.

On the other hand, working for a skilled, focused, and cooperative manager can be invigorating. You can't wait to get to work. Your job is full of opportunities, and you are encouraged to pursue them. You feel appreciated for your successes and are not humiliated by your mistakes.

In every organization, managers must harness the forces of human nature wisely in order to promote the well-being of the organization and the people who give it life. But while nearly 50 percent of all executives believe that poor management is the greatest limitation to the productivity of U.S. companies, we can only point to isolated examples of employers who have changed their ways.

❀ *DON'T ALLOW VENGEANCE*
TO DESTROY PRODUCTIVITY

There's no question that vengeance is the most destructive force, in human nature as well as in companies. It's like a spreading cancer: The cells of a body attack themselves. The cancer takes root when companies ignore the needs of their human workers. It is estimated that employee stress, anxiety, and depression cost employers $23.8 billion annually in absenteeism and lower productivity. Direct medical bills cost another $12.4 billion. Lost earnings from depression-related suicides add another $7.5 billion—an indication of the scope of the tragedy that is played out when managers ignore human values and needs. In the new age at work, the imperative is for managers to stop this cancer from spreading in their own divisions—to demonstrate by action that their companies value their workers highly.

Treating people with respect is not just a matter of virtue, it's also a matter of productivity. With the proper spirit and attitude, it is actually possible to put aside your immediate or long-range problems and, instead, operate in a cohesive and cooperative way in the workplace.

The result is that work becomes an opportunity to marshal the best aspects of oneself: dedication, loyalty, selflessness, intelligence, literacy, creativity, and honest, forthright labor. Not every day at work is an epiphany; certainly countless annoyances erupt from the act of commerce to reduce the pleasures of the workaday world. But by focusing on the opportunities that present themselves rather than on the problems, it is possible to transcend the mundane and reach instead for something better, something that engages the best that each of us has to give.

❖ SHOW COMPASSION

In the story of Achilles, we are given a glimpse of the hero as he might have been. In one small moment, his eyes were opened and his anger and hatred fell away. Moved by the old king's plea for his son's body, Achilles behaved nobly, as he was always meant to do, and thus was elevated. As he embraced King Priam, his thoughts were flooded with warm memories of moments shared between fathers and sons, and compassion enveloped the bitter center of his heart.

Compassion is the basic primal connection—the understanding that what you share with other human beings is always a deeper bond than the enmities that might drive you apart.

The term "Achillean" means great in strength and invincibility—or in wrath. It is the wrath of Achilles in first avenging his insult at Agamemnon's hands and then in avenging Patroclus's death that reveal the two sides of his anger.

His fury at Agamemnon was due to the bitter blow to his ego and the challenge to his strength and character. But he failed to unleash his wrath at the commander in chief, preferring instead to let the gods arrange his revenge.

What Achilles experienced when he learned of Patroclus's death was true wrath—an anger born of equal parts of grief, rage, and self-reproach. He didn't want the gods to intervene. Blood vengeance was his alone. He wanted to find and kill Hector himself and personally strip the armor Patroclus wore off the body of his friend's killer.

9

ARROGANCE

Achilles thinks himself invincible; it is a fatal flaw

THE TWELVE DAYS of the truce pass. The people of Troy mourn their fallen prince. The Greek forces have spent their time well. Achilles has gone from camp to camp with Agamemnon, promising the men victory and prizes and telling them that with the fall of Troy they will soon sail for home.

Now that Achilles has restored his fearsome reputation and agreed to return to the business of fighting the war, Priam fears for the fate of the Trojans, still sealed safe inside their city's massive walls. Craving consensus and hoping for some brilliant idea, he calls a meeting of his council to discuss their options. As they talk about what forces are left and who is still alive to lead them, the council chamber grows quiet. One of the councilors nervously suggests that they abandon Troy in the dark of night and go away to settle in a safe place, far from the Greeks. Angered by the suggestion, Priam orders them to stay and fight on for their city. Shame on those who would run and leave behind their homes, their land, their sacred temples!

Then Priam receives electrifying news. They are not alone against the Greeks. Allies are on their way to support their cause. Priam's nephew, King Memnon, and his Ethiopian army will be there before nightfall to join forces with the Trojans.

Upon the arrival of Memnon and his troops, there is much rejoicing. Priam honors the allies with a great feast and lavish gifts. The celebration continues almost all night. As dawn breaks, Memnon takes charge of the combined armies. The Trojan and Ethiopian soldiers pour out of Troy's gates and ride at full speed toward the black ships of the Greeks.

The Greek forces know full well who is charging at them. Their scouts have followed Memnon's army, sending back reports on its strength, number, weapons, and armament. The Greeks know when Memnon and the Ethiopians arrive outside of Troy and permit them to "slip" into the city. The Greeks have waited nine long years for this moment. Today is their day.

The battle is joined as the Greeks, already deployed and waiting, pour down from every direction on the chariots and foot soldiers of the Trojans and Ethiopians. The Ethiopians and Trojans fight furiously, but although they are brave, they wither before the Grecian onslaught.

Glorious in his new armor, godlike in his boldness and fury, Achilles fights his way through phalanx after phalanx of the enemy, cutting them down with such savagery that his armor becomes drenched in blood and gore. Forcing his way deep into the opposing troops, Achilles finally comes face to face with the Ethiopian king, Memnon. The fighting around Achilles and Memnon stops and arms are slowly put away throughout the battlefield. All the combatants fall into a silent truce and turn to watch the contest between the royal warriors.

Achilles and Memnon circle each other warily as they step away from their chariots. Memnon is still completely unscathed. It is clear that he hasn't fought at all yet today but directed the troops from his chariot instead. Achilles, on the other hand, is exhausted and drenched with sweat. He has fought his way to Memnon. Memnon launches three spears in rapid succession, and Achilles leaps, dances, and dodges away from them. Achilles throws only one spear, but it catches Memnon on his flank and draws first blood. Swords in hand, they engage. Memnon is no match for Achilles, and he is quickly beaten to the ground. As he falls, however, he flings his sword at Achilles and opens a long slash high across his exposed inner leg. Finally, both wounded, both limping in pain, they attack each other with huge stones until the field is clear of all but pebbles.

Each has drawn blood; each has fought valiantly. Exhausted and bleeding, they stagger toward each other, the Ethiopian pulling a knife from his scabbard. He feints to

Achilles' left; Achilles drops to the ground, picks a broken spear up as he rolls, and plunges it into Memnon's chest. The Ethiopian drops the knife. His eyes widen, and he shakes his head in disbelief. Blood spurts from his mouth. Both of his hands reflexively grasp the broken shard of spear sticking from the middle of his chest. He stumbles. He falls.

The Greek troops, some by now watching from their ships, let out a mighty roar. It is clear that with Achilles at the forefront of the battle they cannot be defeated.

Achilles slowly gets up and stands over the fallen Memnon, his terrible armor gleaming red, gold, and silver in the sun. He puts his foot on the dead man's stomach, leans down, and pulls the broken spear from Memnon's chest. He lifts the bloody shaft and holds it high above his head. In that moment of total victory, he feels he is indeed a god. All thought of his mortality and his mother's warnings disappear. He is the great Achilles, larger than life, shaper of his own fate. No force of man can destroy him, and no force of god can fell him. Achilles is invincible!

The next morning, Achilles fights fiercely before the walls of Troy, killing every enemy soldier who dares to challenge him. At last he stands at the very gates of the great walled city, ready to break through the last feeble defenses the enemy is able to mount. Troy is going to fall to Achilles.

The god Apollo is furious at the success of the Greeks, but Zeus has stopped him from doing anything about it.

Apollo looks down from Olympus and sees Achilles standing at the gates of Troy. He is outraged by Achilles' slaughter of the Trojans. Apollo flies from one end of Olympus to the other. Mighty Zeus is nowhere to be found. Sensing his opportunity, Apollo snatches his silver bow and quiver of poisoned arrows and flies down from the heavens.

Hoping to remain undiscovered by Zeus, Apollo decides to stay at a safe distance from the action, so he hides behind a low-lying cloud. Apollo then calls to Achilles, warning him to turn from the gates of Troy or face destruction.

It has been a long day for Achilles; he is wounded and has already lost quite a bit of blood. To turn back now, when the fate of Troy unfolds before him, seems ridiculous. Achilles throws back his head and laughs scornfully. In a mighty bellow, a mixture of rancor and disgust, he warns Apollo to keep his nose out of this; he is in no mood to be trifled with. He holds up the broken spear covered with Memnon's blood and promises to let Apollo taste it, if the great god so desires.

It is a bold threat and a dangerous one. Achilles, in the heat of battle, exhausted, has forgotten reality: Apollo is an immortal god, while he himself is the one vulnerable to the arrows of fate.

The battle before the gates of Troy continues, and Achilles is swept back into combat. As he fights on, Apollo lingers behind the clouds. Suddenly, the god sees his chance. Helen's lover, Paris, appears atop the walls of Troy and fires arrow after arrow at the Greeks. Apollo watches him, amused. Paris may be a great lover for the most beautiful woman on earth, but he is a terrible archer.

Apollo leaps from his cloud and alights unseen next to Paris. As Paris readies his next shaft, Apollo simultaneously notches his own poisoned arrow onto his silver bow, appears in Paris's place, and fires at Achilles. The arrow pierces the special armored plate covering Achilles' heel and bores through to the other side of his foot. Achilles grabs the arrow and tries to pull it out from the front, but the poison has already started to work. He stumbles heavily, staggers forward as he reaches out toward a grinning Apollo, and falls onto his hands.

Achilles looks down at his heel and tries to stop the flowing blood with his hand. He looks up at Apollo and mutters a curse. The poison overwhelms him, his body stiffens, and Achilles crashes to the earth.

Apollo is finally satisfied. Achilles invincible? Where does anyone see Achilles invincible?

Death comes to all mortal men. It is the great equalizer.

A Modern Parable: The Fatal Arrogance

This is the story of Adele, a woman of such great wealth and power that everyone around her deferred to her whims. She considered herself far above the rules of common behavior. In Achilles' world, she would have been a demigoddess.

It wasn't always that way. Born of very ordinary parents, Adele was raised in modest circumstances and struggled all her life to become successful. She was driven by a thirst for wealth, a sense of entitlement that grew out of deep inner forces. She married and divorced two husbands because they did not share her ambition. Even as she reached her forties, moderately successful but alone and far from her dreams, she kept her eyes firmly focused on her goal and never wavered.

Then one day Adele found herself at a local business function. The key speaker, a gray and aging tycoon, was the head of the biggest company in town. Adele listened, enraptured, to his polished, confident presentation. She noticed he had the distinct bearing of a man accustomed to receiving deference from others, and a smooth mastery of the language and gestures of power. Strength of purpose was etched in every line on his face. At the reception that followed, Adele boldly went up and introduced herself. She told him how much his speech meant to her, and he regarded her with intense interest. As their eyes met, something clicked. At last, Adele thought, here is a man who sees things the way I do.

Adele didn't care that the tycoon was thirty years her elder. She had no use for the youthful vitality so many men possessed. Their eagerness to succeed was merely a sign that they had not already succeeded. She was more interested in a man who was comfortable in the skin of power and privilege.

When Adele wanted something, she moved heaven and earth to get it. And this she wanted: to be a part of this man's world. Not only did she want it, she deserved it, was entitled to it. She researched and read every detail she could about his life. She found reasons to be in his presence. She altered her résumé and persona to appear more comfortable with power and wealth than she really was. And although he had been married for many years, Adele managed to disentangle the tycoon from his wife and create discord and separation with relative ease. The wife was elderly and secure; Adele provided a hot spark to the tycoon, making him feel young and alive again.

Once they were married, Adele easily persuaded him that she possessed the talent and ability to be his business partner. She alone could provide a shot of adrenaline for his stodgy empire. Over the objections of his longtime partners and protective staff, the tycoon gave Adele a powerful decision-making position in his company. He made it clear that his wife operated as his eyes and ears; she represented him with full authority.

Within a couple of years, Adele had managed to revamp the entire executive wing of the company, replacing the tycoon's loyalists with people loyal to her. She also promoted estrangements among the tycoon's oldest business partners, accusing them of stock and accounting manipulations that, after years of litigation, were proved false. Adele rose even further and faster than she had anticipated. With the exception of the tycoon himself, who was growing increasingly frail, Adele managed to acquire almost total control of the tycoon's entire company.

Finally she sat in the seat of power, and she loved it. She now controlled the lives of thousands of people. If she wanted things done her way, things would be done her way. It was Adele's way or the highway. That soon meant everyone: If her office wasn't cleaned exactly as she had ordered, she'd have the cleaner fired. If an employee was disrespectful, incompetent, or inefficient in any way, she would have that employee dismissed. This attitude soon extended to every facet of her life. Adele went through housekeepers, gardeners, maids, butlers, and cooks almost faster than they could be provided.

Employee morale at the company plummeted under Adele's leadership. Years of commitment, hard work, and service were suddenly meaningless. Adele made it clear that the only standard was the one she set.

The tycoon was attended by nurses now. He knew little about day-to-day business practices. He trusted his brilliant wife, who had rescued his company during his physical decline. He was grateful to her and she, in turn, spoke often of her deep love for him.

Adele had always been obsessed with the amount of money the company spent in the course of business. She was particularly galled by huge tax payments that totaled millions of dollars every year. It seemed to Adele that the tax payments were excessive, so she began to study the tax laws herself, although she kept a full stable of tax lawyers, auditors, and accountants for that very purpose. Soon she was spending most of her time in the accounting offices, studying the files and making lists of deductions that weren't being claimed—including tens of thousands of dollars in personal receipts. When the head of accounting patiently explained that the company could not claim these as legitimate deductions, she simply fired him on the spot, calling the security force to escort him from the building. Then she replaced him with a man who respected her authority, and he filed taxes according to her instructions.

Her belief in her invincibility complete, Adele assumed that all was well. Her pedestal was so high she could not detect the resentments that raged below. Not surprisingly, an anonymous tipster informed the IRS that Adele was the mastermind behind an enormous tax fraud.

Adele was indignant when the IRS agents came calling. She reminded them of the millions she paid every year. How dare they! But they did dare.

When Adele was put on trial for tax evasion, she complained publicly about government harassment. Her haughty manner, her disdain for the law, her derisive denials of wrongdoing were designed to show the world the true extent of the injustice being perpetrated on her by the IRS. She assumed that everyone, including the members of the jury at her trial, would be outraged at the mistreatment she was receiving. Instead, the public saw a woman consumed with greed and power, a petty tyrant and miser who thought nothing of using her position to cheat and humiliate others. The jury agreed with that assessment. When they announced a verdict of guilty, Adele clutched at her chest as though she'd been stabbed. Suddenly, all the majesty drained out of her face, and she looked old and vulnerable. The verdict was like a death blow that pierced the armor of her arrogance and found the fatal weakness underneath.

Months later, after all appeals were exhausted, Adele was led away to serve a five-year sentence at a federal prison. When a reporter asked her how she felt, she cursed those who had done this to her and vowed to spend the rest of her life finding ways to pay them back. Even at the end, she did not realize that the blame for her downfall rested in her own heart.

Lesson Nine

The Shield of Humility

Connie Bruck, in her riveting tale of corporate drama *Master of the Game: Steve Ross and the Creation of Time Warner* (Simon & Schuster, 1994), wrote of Ross that since he felt "exempt from legal and ethical standards, he abrogated them at will. To violate all these standards, and never to be publicly caught at it—more, to be perceived by thousands as the very exemplar of some of these standards—now *that*, for someone like Ross, was winning."

How many times have we heard the crash of the mighty being felled, seen the greatest of leaders pulled unceremoniously from their pedestals? Even those who seem to have earned the shield of invincibility—for example, the massive conglomerates that control what we read, what we view, and how we communicate—are vulnerable, for they rule only at the pleasure of those they serve. It is all too easy for the leaders of such dominant industries to think their power is infinite and the public will automatically accept the product that bears their logo. But this has never been true, and it's not true today. Those who think their control is unshakable might heed the painful lesson learned by General Motors in the 1970s and 1980s. The company whose motto was "What's good for General Motors is good for the nation" was stunned when "the nation" decided it preferred small cars. If General Motors didn't make them, they'd find them elsewhere—and they did.

Pride isn't necessarily a bad attribute. Indeed, a strong ego and fierce ambition are among the hallmarks of success. Few achieve greatness who are not in some way driven beyond the ordinary.

Arrogance, however, slowly unravels the tight fabric of success. First, there is a loss of perspective, a false sense of invincibility. This is followed by an obsessive need to maintain dominance, even at the expense of loyalty, morality, and productivity. As your world becomes narrower, you begin to abandon friends and colleagues, and they abandon you. Finally, lacking loyal and skilled colleagues and friends to support you, at work or in your personal life, you are left alone in the great "out there"—a target for all. The process may occur over months, or it may take years. But arrogance is always a fatal flaw—precisely because the arrogant among us are unable to comprehend the nature of their mortality.

The new age at work presents us with a choice between arrogance and humility. It is a classic battle, present in every generation, but giant egos can cut a larger swath today. There has never before been a period in history when individuals were able to achieve such phenomenal personal wealth and corporate power, much less control global dynasties, without ever leaving their offices. Humility may be scoffed at by such people as these; as the old saying goes, "It's hard to be humble when you're as great as I." But the primal truth, old as humanity, is that we are all vulnerable to the same mortality, and those who believe themselves immortal often fall harder and faster than others.

Your ninth shield is the armor of humility, crafted from the following:

❖ KEEP YOUR ACCOMPLISHMENTS IN PERSPECTIVE

An arrogant manager can empty a room pretty fast. Boasting, smugness, and a compulsion to succeed at any cost are sure ways to alienate everyone around you. To outperform your peers is laudable. To constantly remind them that you have done so is sheer folly. Vain people have few allies when they are on top and virtually none when their fortunes fall.

When you give your colleagues their full measure of credit for your company's successes, you assure their willing cooperation when you run into problems. They are invested in your success. It belongs to them, not just to you.

❈ GIVE YOUR STAFF REAL AUTHORITY

An arrogant manager believes that he or she alone knows what's best and thus fails to delegate tasks or authority to others. Not only does this attitude denigrate the talents and abilities of the manager's staff and keep them in a place of submission, it's also very bad for the bottom line. In a recent survey of management behavior conducted by Mercer Management Consulting, it was reported that managers at the least profitable companies tended to be less able to delegate than managers at more successful companies. Micromanagement reduced the effectiveness of managers who could put their authority and abilities to better use.

Your subordinates were not hired to make *you* look good. But you *will* look good if you provide them with the direction, resources, and training they need to succeed at their jobs. When they do well, others will take note of your management skills.

On the other hand, if only some of your subordinates

succeed, you will be considered a mediocre manager. And if most of them fail, your reputation will be seriously tarnished. No matter how outstanding your individual contributions are, you will be judged primarily by the skill with which you manage your people and bring out their best efforts. It's a win-win proposition.

❀ RECOGNIZE YOUR LIMITATIONS

Blind ambition blurs the line between reasonable and unreasonable risk. To avoid becoming a victim of your ambition, recognize your mortality—in other words, your limitations. Every endeavor contains both imposed restrictions and natural restrictions. Imposed restrictions include company goals, finite resources, ordinary skills, modest experience, conflicting demands, and inflexible deadlines. Natural restrictions follow the boundaries of your intellectual and problem-solving capabilities, your physical and emotional stamina, and your determination. Your task is to keep all the balls spinning at once—and to recognize the difference between courage and suicide.

Wise leaders appreciate their weaknesses and surround themselves with others who possess the strengths they don't have. If you're compelled to micromanage every task and do not promote others who can complement your gifts, you will be walking a tightrope without a net, no matter how skilled you are.

❀ STAND UP TO ARROGANT COWORKERS

It's sometimes more frustrating than gratifying to manage arrogant but highly talented people. Self-important subordinates overstate their own accomplishments and overvalue their contributions. They demand more time and attention than they really deserve, and they're always seeking approval. They go out of the way to belittle their peers, hoping to enlist your allegiance with them against the others. If you go along to get along, then the strongest —read, the most obnoxious, selfish, and overbearing—of your subordinates will basically call the tune in your work environment. Don't let them.

It may be uncomfortable, but after carefully assessing the situation and choosing the appropriate moment, take these colleagues aside and clearly define your expectations. Make it clear that their performance will be evaluated in part on their ability to get along with others in the group. Remind them that it isn't your job to pass out gold stars like a kindergarten teacher. Encourage them to find satisfaction in their achievements themselves, more than in hearing praise. Go ahead and be forceful, even blunt. Although arrogant people despise personal criticism, they respect strong and forthright managers.

❖ *NEVER FORGET THAT YOUR COMPANY CAN THRIVE WITHOUT YOU*

You may have hit eighty home runs for the company softball team last season and made sales records seven years in a row, but you're still expendable. Everyone is expendable. Always keep in mind that there are batches of eager and talented twenty-four-year-old MBAs waiting for a crack at your job. There may be giant megacorporations circling, eager to swallow your company whole. The point is: Life is unpredictable, so don't get too attached to your chair.

Remain centered and focused, calm and relaxed. Take a deep breath and say quietly to yourself, "If I don't come in tomorrow or the next day, life goes on. Business goes on. They'll survive without me. They may even find a way to do my job that I never thought of."

Respect the fact that, though you may be valuable to an enterprise, even crucial to its success, the enterprise will survive and can thrive without your participation. None of us want to be just a cog in the wheel of life, but neither can we forever be the hub. Companies don't prosper unless they sometimes change gears.

Also heed the lessons of those who thought they were indispensable, only to find themselves abandoned because of their overbearing arrogance—cut off from all support they might have had.

The following story is true, although the subject is unnamed. You might recognize him, or others like him. He was once a very rich and powerful athlete: famous, hand-some, gifted, the husband of a beautiful woman and the fa-ther of lovely children. He played a very popular and demanding game in front of millions of people, and he played it as part of a famous championship team. He was the unparalleled star of his team, but he could not play his sport alone. The star of a team must also don the mantle of a leader, for his gifts could only be fully utilized when he was complemented by teammates who also possessed su-perbly honed skills. Such a star must know that his true greatness lies in helping others achieve greatness.

But even the greatest of heroes can have faults. By his imperious demeanor, his boasting to the press, his indif-ference to his teammates, and his irritating habit of refer-ring to his team's wins in the singular ("*I* didn't think *I* was going to be able to beat them today"), it was obvious that he saw his teammates merely as appendages to his own glory.

In the early days of his career, it didn't seem to matter much. He led his team to victory after victory. He was strong, swift, and powerful—the best who had ever played the game. His teammates didn't *like* him much, but they did like to win, and he was their ticket to success. But as the seasons passed, and the star gradually began to age, he be-came a little slower, a little weaker. There were fewer breathtaking moments. There were costly errors. More losses. It was then the star needed his team to rally behind him if he was to remain invincible on the field. If his teammates failed to get the ball to him, block for him, sacrifice themselves for him, he could be stopped.

Years of arrogance and indifference finally mounted up for our star. It wasn't that his teammates deliberately set him up for failure, it was just that they didn't care much anymore. Their passion and devotion had not been cultivated. Their worth had never been fully acknowledged. As the hero grew slower, they followed his lead. Opponents who could not strike him before, struck him now. When the ball came to him, it was always just a little late, leaving him vulnerable to crushing blows. His blockers still blocked, but not as long and not as hard, allowing the opposition to beat him down again and again. Suffering injury after injury, and concussion after concussion, this great hero was finally forced to leave the game he loved forever.

One could reasonably say that his age brought him down. Athletic prowess doesn't last forever. But it might have been different for our hero had he not been so arrogant. Perhaps he could have retired on his own terms, with the love and respect of his colleagues. Instead, he faded from view with nothing but his trophies to remind him of what he once was—and might have been.

Achilles was the ideal Greek hero, mightiest of warriors, but he was ruled by his passions, and their heat denied him the cunning he needed to avoid the fate of the gods. Arguably the arrow that pierced Achilles' vulnerable heel was launched an eon before, was ultimately the fashion and design of fate, and nothing Achilles might have done would change the course of his life and death. Yet in a metaphorical sense, we see that Achilles contributed daily to his own demise—with his obsessions, his unreined passions, his selfishness, his pride. And it was at the very point when he finally stood tall and declared, "I am a god," that he fell.

AFTERWORD

The battle lives on
in the armor of Achilles

ACHILLES watches the pool of blood widen beneath him. He feels the venom of Apollo's poisoned arrow course through his veins, burning and then numbing as it travels. He tries to rise again, wants to reach the grinning Apollo standing just feet away, but he falls heavily back. Straining for each breath, he mutters a final curse at Apollo. Then, his eyes glistening with tears, his hand reaching for the sky, the great Achilles lets forth a cry of "Zeus!" and dies.

The Trojans give a thunderous cheer as their enemy perishes at last. Apollo flies away, leaving a stunned Paris in his place. The Trojans rush as one for the body of Achilles, preparing to strip him of his wondrous armor and seek revenge on their enemy, the man who killed their beloved Hector.

From across the battleground a bellow of rage is heard. The Trojans turn and see the giant Greek warrior Ajax almost upon them, swinging a war club the size of a tree. He is matched stride for stride by Ulysses. The two furiously attack the Trojans, beating them away from the fallen Achilles. Ajax carries Achilles across the battlefield cradled like a child in his left arm, still swinging the Trojans off with his club. At last, Ajax reaches the Greek encampment. The valiant Ulysses stays behind to force the Trojans back inside their walls. There is a stunned silence among the Greeks as Ajax returns to the ships bearing the body of Achilles. It doesn't seem possible. When Ulysses returns, having successfully driven the Trojans back, he runs to Achilles' tent, still not believing that Achilles has been killed. The troops are openly weeping at their loss.

The sky begins to darken, and a sharp wind blows in from the sea. The wind carries a faint howl, a distant cry of lamentation, that grows with the force of the wind until it is a piercing scream. The Greeks cover their ears and run for shelter as gouts of blood-red rain begin to pour from the sky, interspersed with thunder and bolts of lightning.

Achilles' mother, Thetis, appears over the camp. It is her lamentation and those of her sister sea nymphs that the Greeks are hearing. Thetis, the other nymphs, and the Nine Muses take form around the body of the fallen Achilles and continue to mourn him. For seventeen days and seventeen nights, the howling and the maelstrom continue unabated. The Greeks, numb, full of grief and pain, try to endure.

On the eighteenth day the wind, the rain, and the shrieking end. Achilles, high on his funeral bier, is set ablaze with fat sheep and cattle roasting beneath him as sacrifice. The Greeks circle his bier with weapons raised in tribute, all of them weeping. The funeral bier burns all day and far into the night. At dawn of the next day, they collect his bones and mix them with those of his dear friend Patroclus in a golden urn fashioned by the god Vulcan.

After the funeral feast, the council of chiefs meets and decides to award Achilles' armor to the next greatest of their warriors. Even with Achilles gone, they believe that the sight of his armor will continue to terrify the Trojans and inspire the Greek troops. The decision comes down to either Ajax or Ulysses. In a secret vote, Ulysses wins.

This is a great honor for Ulysses, and a crushing blow for Ajax. The two great warriors now stand in confrontation, and bitterness rises like black fire from the hearts of men who have fought, suffered, loved, and grieved together all these years.

The wrath of Achilles, like a curse, erupts once again over the disposition of his armor. Eventually, Ajax will kill himself because of its maddening effect.

The wrath of Achilles extends beyond his time and wraps its steady hand around the unshaped clay of the future. The legacy of Achilles' flaws lives on. But so too does the transformation of earthly weakness into an invincible shield. No fate can rule which one you choose.

THE NINE SHIELDS
OF IMMORTALITY

1. The Shield of Commitment

Be True to a Core Ideology

Always retain your values, principles, and beliefs. They will guide your actions with more surety than whim, emotion, or desire.

Be Decisive

Make your decisions by being both fair and wise. You may not be able to control the actions of those around you, but your decisiveness will send a clear message about your position.

Stay Loyal to Your People

Let it be known that you can be counted on in both good times and bad. Loyalty is a flawless mirror—it only reflects what is actually there.

Focus on Your Job,
Not on Saving Your Skin

Concentrate on the work at hand. As any Marine will tell you, the moment you start worrying about your survivability, you've stopped taking care of business. When you've stopped taking care of business, you're dead.

Don't Tolerate the Blame
Game from Employees

An atmosphere of backbiting and vituperation is unproductive. Don't create it and don't tolerate it. It is a dark cloud that can make the workplace unbearable.

If You Must Break a Commitment,
Do It Honorably

Treat others with respect, do what you can to repair any damage, and try to leave them better off than when you first made the commitment.

2. The Shield of Selflessness

Share the Rewards

For those who lead and reap the benefits, make sure that those who follow are well taken care of. For those who follow and are rewarded, you return the favor by giving even more cooperation and effort. Consequently, the sharing of reward is a mutual exchange between dual beneficiaries. Both provide value for the reward.

Don't Get Greedy

It's human nature to stuff your pockets with candy when no one's looking—when you're three years old. Grow up. Greed is an uncontrolled response to opportunity. Control yourself.

Never Take What Rightfully Belongs to Others

Some people have trouble making the fine moral distinction between what belongs to them and what belongs to others. Stealing diminishes the object of desire and makes it worthless in the thief's hands.

Promote Social Responsibility

It's easier to keep your head stuck in the sand, both for companies and for individuals. But it's more rewarding to stick your neck out and be a part of the planet.

⊡⊡⊡⊡⊡⊡⊡⊡⊡⊡⊡⊡⊡⊡⊡⊡⊡⊡⊡⊡⊡⊡⊡⊡⊡⊡

Make Sacrifices at the Top

Honor dictates that the first sacrifice, if any need to be
made, should come from those who bear the responsibility
of making sacrifices necessary in the first place.

3. The Shield of Cooperation

Become a Consensus Builder

It's a lot easier to get twelve people to agree on a business proposition if their input on the matter is asked for and valued.

Settle Your Grievances in Private

The phrase "Let us reason together" is most clearly heard and accepted when it is not screamed belligerently in someone's face in a crowded room.

Don't Abuse Your Position

Everyone loathes dictators until they get a chance to play one themselves. Resist the temptation.

Don't Take Criticism Personally

Sometimes people actually do have your best interests at heart. They're not trying to tear you down or humiliate you. They're just trying to get the job done. Don't imagine arrows that aren't there.

4. The Shield of Integrity

Play Fair

Fair play is usually repaid with fair play. When it's not, you can shrug it off. Fair people don't need to play dirty to win. They're too busy focusing on excellence.

Don't Use Your Influence to Betray Others

When you hold forth in a group of people and you're asked your opinion of someone known to you all, don't use that moment to demean the person being spoken of. Although you may hear assent and see smiles, everyone now knows that you may have an opinion of them to be shared when next they are absent. You harm yourself as you harm others.

Guard Against Bullying

If you are able to criticize without demeaning, ask for a result without insult or sarcasm, and use patience and kindness instead of pressure and hostility, you're not a bully. You're a genius.

Never Make Decisions in the Heat of Emotion

Deciding to emigrate to France and join the Foreign Legion after a particularly vicious budget meeting with the boss is a perfect example of decisions made in the heat of the moment. Don't do it.

5. The Shield of Rigor

Stay the Course

Try to name a true success story that involves someone giving up before the job was done.

Rise Above Moodiness

Everyone is entitled to moods. We're human. But when you see one coming, put it in your briefcase and save it for later when you're alone and can really enjoy it.

Morale Building Is Job One

Nurturing a good employee is an act of courtship. Would you ever court a woman or a man by threatening, intimidating, or demeaning them? Don't flowers and smiles and appreciation work much better?

6. The Shield of Flexibility

Never Say Never

Career change, corporate upheavals, future technologies to come. . . . Never say never if you don't know what never might be.

Force Innovation

People who love to work always look for ways to make the job better, to make it simpler, to smooth the edges. Forcing innovation is the attempt to make work aerodynamic, to cut the resistance between force and flow to a degree of nil.

Don't Be Afraid to Admit Mistakes

If you make a mistake, it really is best to just say, "I messed up," and move on. More time is wasted on covering up mistakes than is spent fixing the mistake once it's discovered. Besides, people will really admire you if you take responsibility.

Choose Your Advisers Carefully

The person who you listen to, the person whose advice you follow, is the most important person in your life. At home, of course, that's your significant other. At work, it might be a fellow worker, a boss, or someone else entirely. But find someone. That's the key.

Don't Submit to Fate

Destiny is as destiny does. If you believe you have no control, then you have no control. However, common sense tells us to at least put up a little struggle. Don't submit to your fate. It makes it more fun for the gods when you squirm and wriggle a little bit.

7. The Shield of Honesty

Don't Let Others Take the Fall for You

If you're good enough to be in charge, you're good enough to face the problems head-on. If you can't stand the heat, step aside.

Delegate Authority Responsibly

People are never only judged for how they do their job. People are judged for what jobs they decide the people who work for them should do. The boss's job is to recognize and meld the differences of individuals to maximize everyone's potential.

Be Honest

If someone is doing a lousy job, say so. Don't let him find out when he gets the pink slip in his pay envelope. Honesty is always kinder.

8. The Shield of Respect

Treat Your Workers like Human Beings, Not Machines

Your workers are not interchangeable parts for your big machinery. If you treat them like machines, they'll spend a lot of time out for repairs.

Don't Allow Vengeance to Destroy Productivity

What's more important, killing your obnoxious colleague or scoring that big bucks contract? If you're not sure, ask an objective observer.

Show Compassion

If you can stop thinking about yourself for a moment and look out into the wider world, you may find that there are many others who need love and caring, work and shelter, a kind word, and some decency. Give what you have.

9. The Shield of Humility

Keep Your Accomplishments in Perspective

You really may be the best thing down the pike since Lucky Strike green went to war, but your abilities will seem a lot more daunting if you don't advertise them, but instead quietly, resolutely, modestly perform them.

Give Your Staff Real Authority

The inability to trust the people you work with to do what they are supposed to be doing means that you will never be able to do what *you're* supposed to be doing.

Recognize Your Limitations

You can rush in where wise men fear to tread. You can step onto a busy street without looking out for speeding cars. You can go swimming immediately after eating an enormous meal. You can jump off high mountains. But eventually you're going to land.

Stand Up to Arrogant Coworkers

The best way to do that is to ignore them. Arrogant people hate that. You can also feel sorry for them. Arrogance masks a lot of pain.

Never Forget That Your Company Can Thrive Without You

Any good business worth its salt is created just so it can eventually function like a well-oiled machine even without its founder, creator, director, or in-house genius. Let go when it's time. It's okay to be sad, but then move on.

ABOUT THE AUTHOR

WESS ROBERTS IS the international best-selling author of *Leadership Secrets of Attila the Hun, Straight A's Never Made Anybody Rich, Victory Secrets of Attila the Hun,* and *Make It So* (with Bill Ross). His books have been translated into twenty-five languages.

His professional experience includes senior management positions at American Express Company and Fireman's Fund Insurance Company. He was a project engineer at Northrop Services Company, a project director at Courseware, Inc., and a major in the U.S. Army, where he was assigned for three years to the Combat Arms Training Board. As an adjunct professor at Southern Utah University, Utah State University, and Nova University, he has taught undergraduate and graduate courses in business, education, and psychology.

A noted speaker, he has addressed business, university, association, and government audiences in the United States, Europe, and Asia. He is the recipient of the U.S. Department of the Treasury's Patriotic Service Award, is the executive producer of six award-winning motivation and training films, has authored over forty-five professional papers on human behavior, and is a member of the U.S. Army Field Artillery OCS Hall of Fame.

He currently makes his home in Utah, from where he writes on a variety of business and leadership topics.